THE BLISS PROTOCOL

The Bliss Protocol

Kofie and Lachele Bryant

Copyright © 2024 by Kofie and Lachele Bryant
All rights reserved. No part of this book may be reproduced in any manner whatsoever without written permission except in the case of brief quotations embodied in critical articles and reviews.
First Printing, 2024

Contents

Dedication	v
Acknowledgements	1
Forward	2
1 Family Lyfe	5
2 Cultivating Compassionate Communication	23
3 Bliss	38
4 The Art of Constructive Conflict	54
5 Unity in Intimacy	73
6 Flourishing in Shared Abundance	93
7 Embracing Unified Purpose	109
8 Nurturing Physical and Spiritual Well-being	128
9 Cultivating Mindful Wealth Management	145
10 Cultivating Collective Joy	163
11 Expanding the Circle of Trust	180
12 Building Legacy and Leadership	198

Dedication

To our Parents: (Lachele A. Bryant) Catherine Bethea Dixon, and Melvin and Carolyn Bethea. (Kofie Bryant Sr.) Walter Bryant and Felene Bryant Barnett (R.I.P) and Surrogate parents Jepp & Gloria Milhouse, children (Abena, Kofie Jr. and Nanya Braynt), our host of Blended Family and the generations to come: may you find in these pages the seeds of love, legacy, and leadership to cultivate your own beautiful gardens of partnership and purpose.

To the couples who have walked this path before us, lighting the way with your wisdom and resilience. Your examples have shown us the transformative power of unity in marriage.

To our beloved community Inspired Life Ministries, family, and friends who have nurtured our journey and inspired us to grow together in love and service. Your support and encouragement have been the fertile soil in which our shared vision has taken root and flourished.

And to each other - Kofie and Lachele - for the dance of love, growth, and shared dreams that have brought us to this moment. Our journey together is our greatest blessing and adventure.

Acknowledgements

We are profoundly grateful to:

Our spiritual mentors and guides have helped shape our understanding of marriage as a sacred calling and vehicle for transformational change in the world.

The countless couples who have shared their stories, struggles, and triumphs with us, enriching our perspective and deepening our compassion.

To our Team/Tribe Black CEO: Trevor Otts, E.R Spaulding, Tiffany B., Christy S., and Vitaliy V. To name a few, their guidance and Accountability Partnership are immeasurable and necessary for our success!

Our editors and publishing team at Bethune Publishing House, Inc. for their expertise and dedication in bringing this labor of love to fruition. Also a special thanks to Mark and Kim Robinson from MK Photography for capturing and freezing some of our best moments on film!

The organizations and communities that have provided opportunities for us to serve, lead, and grow together, such as Aaron's Hope (Supporting individuals with Autism Spectrum Disorders) with Founder and Author of " Mimmy's Secret " Adriane McCann

Our families, have surrounded us with love and supported our vision from the very beginning.

Above all, we give thanks to our Divine Source Jesus the Christ, that has blessed our union and continues to give life to our assignments and bring love and purpose to our path together.

Forward

Written by Trevor Otts
Founder and CEO of BlackCEO, Inc.

I have a fire in my belly and a song in my heart, for I have been blessed to witness the birth of something extraordinary. "The Bliss Protocol: How to Save Your Marriage, Find Joy, and Have Peace" by Kofie and Lachele Bryant isn't just a book—it's a revelation, a roadmap to the Promised Land of marital harmony and community leadership!

Can I get an amen?

Now, let me tell you something. In this world of hustle and grind, where we're all chasing that next dollar, that next deal, that next level of success, we often forget the most important currency of all—love. Oh, but Kofie and Lachele, they haven't forgotten. No, sir! They've taken that love, wrapped it in wisdom, dipped it in faith, and served it up on a platter of hope for all of us to feast upon.

You see, these two servants of God understand something that many of us have yet to grasp. They know that true wealth, true power, true success isn't measured by the size of your bank account or the square footage of your house. It's measured by the impact you make, the lives you touch, and the legacy you leave behind.

And let me tell you, family, this book is dripping with that kind of wealth!

Now, I know some of you are thinking, "But Trevor, what does a book about marriage have to do with my business? What does it have to do with my hustle?" Well, let me break it down for you. Everything—and I mean everything—starts with your foundation. And there's no foundation stronger than a marriage built on God's principles, no partnership more powerful than one forged in the fires of love and mutual respect.

The Bryants have laid out a blueprint, a divine strategy if you will, for not just surviving in your marriage but thriving. And when you thrive in your marriage, oh child, you thrive in every area of your life!

But it doesn't stop there. Oh no, it doesn't stop there! This book takes you beyond the four walls of your home and into the streets of your community. It shows you how to take that love, that unity, that power you've cultivated in your marriage and use it to lift up your neighbors, to inspire your brothers and sisters, to be a beacon of hope in a world that desperately needs it.

Can you feel the power in that? Can you see the potential?

This, my friends, is what true leadership looks like. This is what it means to build a legacy that will outlive you, that will echo through the generations long after you're gone.

So I challenge you today. No, I dare you. I dare you to pick up this book and let its words seep into your soul. I dare you to apply its principles to your life, to your marriage, to your business. I dare you to become the leader, the partner, the change-maker that God created you to be.

Because when you do, when you embrace "The Bliss Protocol," you're not just changing your life. You're changing your family. You're changing your community. You're changing the world!

So are you ready? Are you ready to step into your destiny? Are you ready to embrace the bliss, the blessings, and the breakthrough that God has in store for you?

Then open this book, my friends. Open it with expectation. Open it with faith. And watch as God uses the words of Kofie and Lachele Bryant to transform your life from the inside out.

This is your moment, your time, your "Bliss Protocol." Embrace it, live it, and share it.

May God bless you abundantly as you do.

Trevor Otts

1
Family Lyfe

His, Mine, Ours

Bethune Graphics

Crafting Harmony Within Blended Families

PRINCIPLE: "Harmony in diversity fosters unity in love"
BLISS PROTOCOL #10: Embracing Difference:

- Scenario: Conflict over differences
- Solution: Difference appreciation
- Implementation: Strength finding
- Key Advice: Use differences as assets

Gather around the table of life, where the feast of family is rich with the spices of our histories and the sweetness of our hopes for the future. As we partake in this meal of matrimony, our hearts, like our hands, are full – full of the dreams we carry for our blended families. Here, within these pages, we embark on an odyssey, a sacred journey that celebrates the confluence of streams into a mighty river, one that flows with the power of unity and the gentle grace of love.

This harmonious blend is not simple; it is not achieved without effort, for it is the art of merging worlds, histories, and hearts. It demands our deepest patience, as time weaves its tapestry from different threads of experiences; our understanding, as we learn the languages of new kin; and our unconditional acceptance, as we embrace each unique soul that comes to sit at the family table.

In the heart of the home where love dwells, we shall explore this principle of creating harmony within diversity. It is as essential to our spirit-filled homes as the very air we breathe, a guiding star in the constellation of our shared lives. As we traverse these topics together, from the rich traditions we carry in our cultural vessels to the boundaries that guard our peace, expect an awakening—an unveiling of what life in a blended family can truly be.

Who are we but the conductors of our familial orchestra, ensuring that every note, though different in pitch and tone, contributes to the symphony of our existence? We are set to learn the graceful dance of joining our steps with those of others - those we once called strangers but now call family.

Our passage will reveal the power of setting firm ground upon which everyone can stand with respect - a blueprint for boundaries that brings order to potential chaos. We shall also navigate the seas of expectations, those silent pressures that weigh heavy on shoulders already burdened with the task of blending. Our compass is understanding, and our map is drawn with the ink of unyielding dedication to each other.

Adversity, that relentless storm, will evaluate our anchors, and it is here we shall learn about the strength stored within the depths of our union. We will learn to build bridges, not walls when words fail us, and through understanding, we forge pathways to peace within our families.

The finale of our quest in this opening chapter will be an affirmation of unity, a declaration of our commitment to the family we have chosen and the love that has chosen us. Together, let us unfold the pages of this chapter, not just with the anticipation of knowledge but with the fervent hope of transformation.

So, dear reader, let this chapter serve as a mirror—a reflection of where you stand and a window to where you shall go. Each word, each sentence is a step on this journey, a guide through the sometimes tangled, yet always beautiful garden of blended family life. Embrace the promise that awaits you: a home filled with the melodies of different hearts singing the same song of unity and love.

As we delve deeper into this experience, let each section be a stone on the path to a harmonious home. May your heart resonate with the love and wisdom contained within, and may we all find, in the chorus of combined souls, the peaceful home for which we yearn.

Transitioning into the next section, let us carry forth the principles learned here and weave them into the intricate and beautiful Tapestry of Traditions—a legacy that honors the past enriches the present, and paves the way for a future bright, inclusive and joyous. Join me as we step into the rich heritage that each member brings to the table, a celebration of the diversity that is the cornerstone of our unity.

The Tapestry of Traditions

Understanding the Tapestry of Traditions within our blended families is akin to gathering a quilt sewn with the threads of our individual pasts. It becomes a shelter, a story in fabric, speaking of our ancestry, successes, and struggles. In this vibrant patchwork, each square is a testament to the rites, rituals, and recipes that flavored our youth, now shared, and merged within the embrace of newfound kinship.

In the warmth of our joined families, we recognize that traditions are not just practices but pillars of our identity. As custodians of legacy, we possess the power to honor these sacred echoes from our predecessors while making room for new symphonies to arise. It is in the blending of these customs we find a new melody harmonizing the old with the new, creating a unique composition that belongs to us all.

Imagine the beauty of Thanksgiving, where an array of dishes from collard greens to jollof rice grace the table, each dish narrating a lineage, each bite a story of triumph and fellowship. Visualize the joyous medley of Kwanzaa, Juneteenth, or Watch Night, enriched by the added layers of new celebrations that add vibrancy to our collective spirit. Together, we establish traditions that honor all members of our tapestry, inclusive of every shade and texture of the families we unite.

Yet, in this creative space of merging, patience is the loom on which we weave our story. Understanding is the shuttle that carries the thread through the warp, and unconditional love – that which binds and heals – is the pattern emerging from every shared moment. It requires a delicate balance, akin to a dance where every step is thoughtful, every turn a celebration of another's rhythm and beat.

To navigate this elegant waltz of convergence, we must listen – truly listen – to the narratives wrapped within each tradition. We shall proceed by sharing stories, folklore, and the heartfelt testimonies of days bygone, cherishing each as a precious heirloom to be preserved and perpetuated. By doing so, we not only respect the paths that have led each of us here but also craft a collective history for generations to carry forward.

Now, as we come together beneath the vast sky of our shared dreams, we must also embrace the creation of new traditions. These are the milestones and annual celebrations that will become the shared memories of tomorrow, the new threads added to our ever-expanding quilt. From family nights to communal service initiatives, these are the occasions that will further knit our hearts together, forging bonds as strong as steel yet as tender as a caress.

Let the rituals we develop be the pillars of our resilience and the hearth of our joy. Let every birthday celebrated, every graduation cheered, and every milestone acknowledged be a golden thread in the rich tapestry we are weaving, affirming that though we originate from disparate shores, we sail together on the same powerful vessel of family unity.

In the spirit of creating this shared tapestry, let our next steps lead us toward understanding the blueprint of boundaries, for as much as we embrace the blending of traditions, we must also navigate the delicate matrix of respect and space. Just as each pattern on a quilt has its shape and definition, so too must our personal and collective boundaries be defined, that harmony may continue to thrive amidst our conjoined lives.

Lachele's Personal Story

I recall a particular Thanksgiving that illuminated the complexities of blending families and traditions. As part of a blended family where my husband has three children from his first marriage, I found myself navigating unfamiliar waters of family customs.

Our oldest stepdaughter called this Thanksgiving, offering to bring a dish to our celebration. Without much thought, I declined her offer, adhering to my longstanding tradition of preparing everything myself when hosting. Only later did I realize the significance of what I had done.

This moment opened my eyes to the rich tapestry of traditions that each family member brings to our blended unit. I hadn't considered that our stepdaughter might have her own cherished customs from before our families merged. This realization was a turning point for me.

Through this experience, I learned the vital importance of honoring the diverse traditions and values each family member contributes to our blended family. It taught me the beauty of creating new family traditions that incorporate elements from all our backgrounds.

Now, as we continue to build and strengthen our blended family, I'm grateful for the opportunity to embrace a more inclusive approach. Whether it's for Thanksgiving dinner or any family gathering, I've learned to welcome contributions from all family members, recognizing that each dish or tradition adds a unique flavor to our shared experiences.

This lesson in flexibility and inclusivity has become a cornerstone in how we celebrate and honor each member of our blended family, creating a richer, more diverse tapestry of traditions for us all.

The Blueprint for Boundaries

The confluence of hearts within a blended family occurs in a space where each is allowed to thrive within their own precinct, where the sanctity of individual boundaries is as revered as collective harmony. Think of it as the skilled crafting of a mosaic, where each distinct piece retains its character, contributing to a larger stunning image when viewed from a distance.

In our lovingly intertwined lives, boundaries function as gentle guides, as the cords that delineate our sacred spaces. They are the silent sentinels, guarding the privacy and respect that each relationship inherently deserves. When properly set, they demarcate a place of trust, an understanding that, even in the closest of bonds, there is room for self. Indeed, that room is essential, for in it we find the quiet where our personal histories can be honored, and our individual dreams can take the shape of plans.

It is within this framework that we navigate the intricacies of relationships with in-laws and former partners - those established trees in the gardens of our lives. Like gardeners, we prune with care, ensuring that while every plant has room to flourish, no single branch overarches to the shadowing of another. This delicate process requires open, honest conversation, wherein each voice is heard and acknowledged. There must exist a transparency of intentions, a clarity of needs that allows for a peaceful coexistence, where the rights of each are upheld by the collective will to respect one another.

In the establishment of these boundaries, the sturdiness of communication cannot be overstated. It forms the cornerstone of this blueprint for it is through the art of dialogue that we express our desires and fears. In sharing our expectations – and being receptive to the needs of others – we lay the bricks of understanding, upon which strong family ties can endure.

But let us not forget, amid structuring these boundaries, the call for flexibility. For as the winds of life blow, shifting the sands beneath us, so too must we adapt the lines we draw. Let love be the compass that guides these adjustments, ensuring that while boundaries protect, they do not become impenetrable walls that divide. Where compassion dictates, let the gates open wide to the solace and support of family.

As we each tend to the gardens within us, we must also look outward, to the gardens we cultivate together – those of our children, who watch and learn from our every deed. In upholding boundaries, we teach them respect; in adjusting them, we model grace. And when it is time for them to plant their gardens, they'll remember the balance and beauty they witnessed, the harmony drawn from diversity, and the borders drawn with love.

Embracing the blueprint for boundaries, our hearts are then prepared to sail further – to navigate those seas of expectations that touch upon our shores with each tidal wave of extended family interactions. Let us chart a course that holds true to the unity we cherish and the growth we aspire to, always steering with the compass of understanding and the map of mutual respect.

Kofie's Personal Story

Reflecting on this chapter brings to mind the profound journey of building our blended family. Each of us entered this new union with a complex tapestry of relationships - previous in-laws, children from past partnerships, and a network of connections forged before our paths converged.

Suddenly, I found myself embracing a new family dynamic: a new mother-in-law, father-in-law, and an extended family of cousins, brothers, and sisters whom I needed to know on a deeper level. Simultaneously, my wife was tasked with forming bonds with my children, ex-partners, and what we might call 'surrogate in-laws' from my side of the family.

This transition wasn't always smooth sailing. Some relationships blossomed easily, while others required more nurturing. We consciously chose to cultivate these new intimate connections, recognizing their importance in our shared life. For me, gaining a mother-in-law filled a void left by the absence of my biological mother. For my wife, who didn't have biological children at the time, these new relationships fulfilled her maternal instincts as she instantly became a mother to three.

As we forged these new bonds, we had to navigate the delicate balance of respecting existing boundaries while establishing new ones.

We faced the challenge of merging different family traditions, overcoming the natural inclination to cling solely to the values and customs we were raised with. Instead, we worked to create new family traditions that honored both our backgrounds.

One of our biggest hurdles was determining who to turn to for support during marital issues or family crises. We had to learn how to handle challenges together while respecting each other's traditions and family dynamics.

These were the pivotal aspects we had to navigate in our blended family experience. It was a journey of growth, compromise, and ultimately, the creation of a rich, diverse family tapestry that honors our past while embracing our shared future.

Navigating the Seas of Expectation

In the vast waters of our joined lives, where the ebb and flow of familial ties draw us closer or nudge us gently apart, navigating the seas of expectation requires a masterful steering of the heart. Here, we acknowledge the winds of hope, desire, and obligation that each family member brings to our convoy, recognizing that these invisible forces shape our collective voyage, much like the unseen currents that guide the ocean's depths.

This journey calls for captains of great wisdom and courage, willing to raise the sails of understanding and adjust the rudders of compromise. In these ever-shifting waters, where stormy expectations can sometimes swell into squalls, we invoke the spirit of empathy. It whispers to us that true navigation lies not in charting a straight course, but in the artful dodging of the waves and the skillful use of the wind, making the most of what the heavens provide.

A family's expectations may rise like mighty cliffs against the sky – majestic to behold, but perilous should we venture too close. Whether it's the cultural insistence on specific rites of passage, or the pressure to maintain certain appearances, we must steer our kinship with both eyes open. We chart our own course, set our own speed, and choose our destinations, guided by the stars of our values and the compass of our joint aspirations.

The pressures given to us by extended family – those keepers of our larger circle – can often feel as though we are navigating through narrow straits, the rocks of tradition and the whirlpools of 'how things are done' threatening to ensnare us. Here, gentle dialogue paired with assertive grace becomes our beacon, illuminating a path that respects both where we have come from and where we yearn to go. It is the language of inclusion, infusing the old maps with new points of interest that reflect the diversity and potential of our collective dreams.

Let us remember, though, as we set sail to meet these expectations, the anchor of reality that grounds us. There are limits to the burdens our vessel can carry, and we must be vigilant not to overload its decks. It is the wisdom of balance and the admission of our limitations that will keep our ship buoyant, avoiding the depths of resentment and the wrecks of strained relationships.

As we man the helm together, with trust as our lookout and patience as our helmsman, we prepare to meet the horizons with a sense of adventure and the tranquility of knowing that our ship will weather the journey. Faith in ourselves and our loved ones becomes the lighthouse guiding us back home, time and again, to safe and loving shores.

For as we navigate these seas of expectation, we weave the stories of our legacy – tales of how we maneuvered through storms, basked in the sunshine, and danced in the rain – leaving a wake of memories in our path that speak to the strength and unity of our family's bond. In these shared experiences, a treasury of trust is built, one that underpins the bridges we construct, leading us toward understanding and fertile ground for growth.

With courage in our hearts and our sights set on the horizon, let us sail forward into the waters that foster understanding, where the varied languages of love and relation are waiting to be discovered. Our voyage through the seas of expectation is but one leg of the beautiful odyssey we embark on together, an odyssey wherein every day is an opportunity to turn tides, open hearts, and explore the infinite potential of the family spirit.

Anchoring in Adversity

In this voyage of intertwined destinies, life's grand ship is sometimes tossed upon fierce and untamed seas. Adversity, like a tempest, can bear down upon our union with gales of misunderstanding and torrents of discord. It's within these squalls that our collective resilience is assessed, and we must find our anchor in the form of fortitude, forgiveness, and an unfaltering empathy for our kin.

Storms will come, as they do in any journey worth its salt, but let not our hearts be troubled. For like sturdy oaks with roots entangled deep in ancestral soil, we are stronger than we appear. In the moments when dark clouds gather and lightning cracks the sky, we cling to the wisdom that even the mightiest storm will pass. The light will pierce the tumultuous clouds, revealing once again the azure canvas of endless possibilities.

Our anchor in these times is our ability to embrace, to hold one another in a silent covenant that speaks louder than the tempest's roar. We say, without words, "I am here. You are not alone." And in this sacred embrace, we find solace and the strength to rebuild the sails that have been battered by winds of contention.

Forgiveness is the balm that heals the sores of conflict. A gift we bestow not just upon those who have weathered the storm with us, but upon ourselves. As we give this gift freely, we are unshackled from the heavy chains of past mistakes, our vessel lightened and ready to sail the calm seas with a rejuvenated spirit.

Yet, empathy must be the compass that steers us through these choppy waters. When we look into the eyes of another, particularly those we call family, let us see the reflection of our own humanity. Let us understand that each wave of challenge or moment of friction has underneath it a hidden pearl of insight into the other's soul, waiting to be discovered and cherished.

In unity, we draw from the deep well of our shared legacy – the stories of ancestors who knew the weight of struggle and the lightness of hope. It is these same stories that embolden us, stories of triumph that whisper in our ears whenever the seas grow wild and the gales surge, reminding us that we, too, possess the power to persevere.

As we look to the horizon, we recognize that while we cannot control the storm, we can adjust our sails. It is in these adjustments, these small acts of patience and understanding, that the true nature of our journey reveals itself. It is not merely the destination we seek, but the way we navigate the voyage – together, united, a chorus of many voices singing the same soulful hymn.

We emerge from each tempest not as fragmented driftwood, but as a ship crafted anew, its hull fortified by the wisdom of shared experience, ready for the waters that lie ahead. And as we cast our gaze upon the stillness after the storm, we find a renewed sense of purpose, an invigorated commitment to harmony – one that holds the promise of fair winds and following seas.

Thus, when adversity's gales do quiet and the skies brighten into the soft hues of dawn's grace, we prepare ourselves for the next passage of our expedition – one marked by understanding, compassion, and the art of connection that binds us all. With each sunrise, we renew our pledge – to be beacons of empathy and pillars of mutual support, always pushing forward, past the edge of the horizon, into the unfolding narrative of our shared life.

Building Bridges of Understanding

Like the quiet dawn that joins land and sky in a tapestry of light, understanding is the bridge that connects disparate shores of experience and perspective in our blended families. Carefully constructed with the timbers of patience, empathy, and genuine conversation, these bridges offer passage over turbulent rivers of miscommunication and discord, guiding us toward a communal sanctuary of acceptance and unity.

Active listening, that sacred act of true hearing, serves as the cornerstone of our bridge. It is not merely an absence of speech but an embrace of another's words, an acknowledgment of their intrinsic value in our shared existence. Through this art, the symphony of our loved ones' hopes, fears, and dreams resonate within us, not as echoes but as original compositions that enrich the harmony of our collective narrative.

Empathy is the light that guides each step across the bridge. It implores us to walk in the shoes of another, to feel the texture of their experiences beneath our soles, and to see the world through their eyes. When we employ empathy, we transcend the boundaries of self, and our hearts become attuned to the emotional rhythms of those we love. This sacred resonance transforms every interaction into an opportunity for deeper connection and profound insight.

Communication becomes the handrails of our bridge, granting us the support to traverse the span with confidence. It is through the clarity of transparent dialogue that misunderstandings are unraveled, and the strength of our bond is fortified. But communication is more than the precision of language; it is the courageous vulnerability of sharing our innermost selves, the tender offering of our truths to one another.

Within this section, we offer not simply theoretical musings but practical steps, and tangible exercises that can be plied like well-worn tools in the crafting of these vital connections. From the gentle repetition of a loved one's words, affirming their message has been heard, to the deep reflective pause that gives space for empathy to flourish, these are the rituals that build the fortress of our familial understanding.

Let us also remember that true understanding celebrates not just the consonance but the dissonance, the uniqueness of everyone's melody within our collective song. These diverse verses are not to be silenced but rather blended in respectful symphony - for in their distinction, we create a richer, more vibrant composition that honors the full spectrum of our shared humanity.

With understanding firmly anchored within our hearts, our eyes turn towards the horizon, where the dawn of affirmation awaits. This luminous horizon is not a distant, untouched shore, but rather a place that we have actively carved out in the here and now, through our commitment to unity and our dedication to one another's well-being.

So, let us continue this journey, each step upon the bridge, a testament to the love and respect that sustains us. With each gentle word, each empathetic gesture, and every open-hearted exchange, we take one stride closer to that place of mutual understanding and ceaseless support.

Every bridge built is a legacy in itself – a testament to the work of many hands and hearts, united in purpose and strengthened by each shared triumph and challenge. As we reach the close of this chapter, a new chapter beckons, one that is rooted in the affirmations we pronounce today, for a future resplendent with the joys and victories of a family woven together in the unbreakable bonds of understanding.

Affirmation of Unity

In the quilt of our collective existence, each stitch that binds us is a testament to our shared commitment to unity. This patchwork of many textures, colors, and patterns comes together in a harmonious design, much like a chorus whose diverse voices blend to create a single, soaring melody. As we stand upon the bridge of understanding, looking back at the steps we've traversed, let us now declare an affirmation of unity that serves as the beacon for our future.

In this sacred space, we echo an affirmation that resounds with the depth of our sincerest intentions. We affirm to hold the threads of our love with tender care, to strengthen them through our actions and chosen words, ensuring they weather the most formidable of storms. Our pledge is one of mutual respect, a commitment to see the divine spark within each soul that gathers at our table, honoring the individual journeys that have woven into our shared tapestry.

As we affirm unity, we recognize that each member of our blended family is as crucial as the cornerstones of a majestic arch. Without any one of us, the integrity of our structure might falter, and so we celebrate the unique contributions that each of us brings. Together we stand, an embodiment of strength, each of us supporting and being supported in the fullness of trust and humility.

This affirmation also acknowledges the importance of grace - that essential element that allows us to forgive freely and love unconditionally. We understand that to err is human, to forgive, divine, and within our home, grace flows as abundantly as the warmth of the sun. It is the salve that helps heal old wounds and the light that leads us out of the shadow of past grievances.

Our union is not merely about coexistence but about cultivating a joyful sanctuary where dreams are nurtured, and spirits soar. Here, laughter is our shared language, and compassion, our currency. We create a realm where every victory is celebrated with gusto and even the smallest triumphs are met with praise and jubilation.

Each day, we choose to intertwine our lives with an unwavering commitment to the well-being of our loved ones. We vow to uplift each other, to provide a steadfast foundation from which we can all grow and flourish. In this environment of shared love and dedication, we enable everyone to rise and, in turn, lift the collective spirit of our household.

Acknowledging the labors and triumphs that have carried us to this point, we look towards a horizon aglow with the promise of fulfilled dreams and harmonious living. We embrace the power of our affirmation of unity, allowing it to guide us as a family shield and emblem of courage through the path we walk together.

And as the chapter of our journey continues, each line we scribe in our story becomes a verse in a grander poem of love. We turn the pages, eager to unfold the narrative that lies ahead, knowing that within each word, action, and moment together, we write our own destiny.

So, let us carry the torch of this affirmation into the next chapter of our lives and embrace the serenity that comes from knowing we are surrounded by a love that is indefatigable, resilient, and eternal. Onward we move, hearts united, spirits aligned, to a place we call BLISS, where the cultivation of serenity in a spirit-filled home awaits us with open arms and an infinite well of hope and joy.

2

Cultivating Compassionate Communication

Communication of the Heart

MK Photography

Bridging Hearts Through Empathy and Understanding

PRINCIPLE: "True understanding stems from the heart's ability to listen; compassionate communication forges unbreakable bonds of spiritual intimacy."

BLISS PROTOCOL #2: The Art of Intentional Listening

- **Scenario:** Surface-level communication
- **Solution:** Deep listening practices
- **Implementation:** Active listening exercises
- **Key Advice:** Listen for heart behind words

In the dance of dialogues that is marriage, the music is made not just in the speaking but in the listening. It is in the sacred pause between the notes, where the heart tunes in to hear the unspoken symphony of a partner's soul. "That Marriage Lyfe" opens its arms to you, inviting you into a realm where words are more than mere sounds—they are heartbeats. They pulse with the lifeblood of connection, empathy, and understanding.

This chapter is an odyssey that begins in the rich soil of attentive silence, where you learn that to cultivate a bond that thrives, you must first address the whispers of your partner's heart. As we trace the contours of each other's inner landscapes through empathetic dialogue, we are sowing the seeds for a harvest of trust, a fertile ground where love can bloom in resplendent hues.

Our journey through this chapter promises a beacon of light amidst the twilight of misunderstood silences. Here, we will gently unfurl the petals of your listening spirit, nurturing it with the sunrays of intention and the water of patience.

Let us embark on this exploration together, with the reassurance that in mastering the art of listening with the heart, every syllable spoken becomes a thread in the tapestry of a marriage profound and divine.

Imagine a world where every conversation is a brushstroke on the canvas of your united destiny—where disputes become dialogues, and silence is laden with meaning. With each tender nod, every unhurried response, we are building a fortress against the ephemeral storms of life.

This is the promise of compassionate communication: a love so fluent in its spiritual intimacy that it becomes a language unto itself, understood without words.

As we transcend the ordinary, we find ourselves awakening to the extraordinary—the truth that in the echo chamber of human connection, our hearts are the most resonant of all.

Through this principle of soulful listening, we awaken to the symphony of our shared existence, each harmonic a vibrant note in the melody of matrimonial harmony.

In the coming sections, we will delve into the sanctity of unveiling the heart, navigating the sacred, mirroring understanding, weaving intimacy, and the languages of love. Through this exploration, we will paint a landscape where each emotion expressed, and each desire understood, becomes a brushstroke of intimacy, creating a masterpiece that is uniquely ours.

As we set the stage for this journey, remember that the path ahead is paved with the gold of your willingness to truly hear and be heard. With each step, anticipate not just the knowledge imparted but the transformation that awaits. For it is through the gateway of the heart that we find the truest form of connection—one that echoes through the chambers of time and resonates within the souls of all who dare to love deeply.

As you inhale the ensuing wisdom, permit it to settle in your bones, to resonate through your being. May it prepare you for the unveiling of the heart—the sacred unraveling that follows when we dare to listen, truly listen, to the whispers of love spoken in the quiet corners of our shared journey.

Let us move forward, together, into the embrace of mutual discovery and the affirmation of a connection that comes from the most profound listening of all—listening with the heart.

Unveiling the Heart: Overcoming Emotional Barriers

Imagine a garden where every flower is a word spoken, every leaf an emotion felt, and every root a thought unexpressed. In the lushness of connection lies the possibility of understanding, but beneath the surface, the soil can harden with the rocks of unresolved feelings and words left unsaid.

Here, in Unveiling the Heart: Overcoming Emotional Barriers, we till the soil of our soul's garden, removing those rocks and tending to the delicate sprouts of our innermost emotions.

It is a universal experience—those moments when the heart swells with words trapped behind the dam of apprehension or hurt. The flow of true communion is blocked, leaving partners feeling like islands in a shared space. And yet, the power to break these walls lies within the same forces that built them: our thoughts, our emotions, and our will to transcend.

Within these pages, you will find solace and tools—the soft light of dawn that promises a new day of understanding. As we embark on this excavating journey, you will uncover strategies that free the voice within, and help you articulate the sentiments that grip your spirit with a tender, yet unassailable strength.

It is about creating sacred spaces where vulnerability is honored, and emotions are welcomed with the reverence of heartfelt devotion.

We navigate the labyrinth of feelings, acknowledging the shadows of past misunderstandings while kindling the flame of present awareness. Envision a dialogue that isn't a battle to be won but a dance to be shared, each step a mutual progression toward mutual comprehension and respect. It is in the act of baring our souls that we offer the gift of our truth, and in the act of receiving, we are granted the privilege to see and be seen.

The commitment to overcome these emotional barriers is akin to unwrapping a precious heirloom, one layer at a time. It's in the gentle peeling back of these wrappings that we reveal the beauty of our truest selves and the depth of our love.

Together, we carve out a haven of trust—a place where the whispers of our hearts are loud, where our silences speak as eloquently as words, and where the touch of a hand says, "I am here; I understand."

With each memory shared and each fear acknowledged, you grow closer, your roots intertwining in the rich earth of shared experience. Here you will learn the delicate art of emotional alchemy, transforming the base metals of hurt, jealousy, or anger into the gold of compassion, closeness, and empathy.

As our journey in this oasis of insight nears its resting point, we prepare to carry forth the elixir of understanding into ever more sacred terrains. The conversations that once seemed treacherous now beckon with the promise of richer connection and deeper resonance, the soul's language now a wellspring of love's most eloquent expressions.

In the spaces between, where the heartbeat of your bond sits awaiting the warmth of acknowledgment, the earth is tilted, the flowers bloom, and the garden of your union flourishes. Let this growing sanctuary of connection fill you with anticipation for the deeper exploration to come, as we step into the vastness of the spirit, ready to navigate the ebbs and flows of spiritual conversations with the map of openhearted courage.

Sacred Dialogues: Navigating Spiritual Conversations

The threads of spirit and faith weave through the heart of marriage, a pattern intricate and infinite. In "Sacred Dialogues: Navigating Spiritual Conversations," we embrace the delicate nature of these threads, acknowledging their strength in the tapestry of our union. As we journey deeper into the sanctuary of our shared life, the sacred ground upon which we both tread beckons us to hold space for the spiritual essence that animates our bond.

Imagine standing at the confluence of two rivers, each one representing the spiritual journey of a soul mate. Here, the waters may sometimes swirl turbulently, their courses mingling as they seek to find harmony in their flow. Engaging in spiritual conversations is the vow to navigate these waters with reverence, to honor the distinct paths that have shaped the beliefs cradled within us. It requires an openness of mind, a softness of heart, and a courageous vulnerability that ventures beyond the boundaries of our own knowing.

In this shared pilgrimage, it is not our aim to carve the other into our image but to witness, with awe, the divine reflection that each brings to the altar of our togetherness. When we speak of faith, we speak not just of doctrines or scriptures but of the lived experiences, the quiet revelations, and the inner awakenings that our journeys have granted us. These dialogues become a dance of sacred storytelling—a rhythm that pulses with the beats of our deepest convictions.

Let us navigate these dialogues with the tender steps of empathy, the gentle gaze of understanding, and the embrace of unconditional love. As we traverse the landscape of our spiritual selves, let the exchange of our truths be a journey not toward persuasion, but toward elevation—a shared ascension to heights yet unknown, where the panorama of our unity is breathtakingly clear.

Such sacred dialogues call for the patience of the eternal, the wisdom that time itself unravels. In this communion of spirits, we may find ourselves at a crossroads, faced with views that challenge or confound our own. It is here, in these moments of heartfelt exchange, that we anchor ourselves in the trust we have cultivated, the respect that forms the bedrock of our love.

The willingness to explore together, to sometimes agree to walk hand in hand in the mystery of the unknown, forges in us a connection that transcends the mundane. It binds us in a fellowship that is as profound as the whisper of prayer in the still of the night, as enduring as the faith that has weathered the storms of life.

As we hold this course, let us celebrate the beauty that emerges when two souls are brave enough to share their innermost sanctuaries. Let the dialogue be both a journey and a destination, where the lines of dogma fade into a horizon lit by the light of mutual adoration and the shared seeking of truths larger than ourselves.

And so, as we gently fold the pages of these dialogues, we ready our hearts for the reflective pools that await us. Beyond the hallowed chapters of spiritual exchange lies a realm where understanding is mirrored not just in the words we speak but in the responses we give to one another. With spirits attuned and hearts wide open, we forge ahead to discover the mirror of understanding, where love's reflection is the truest guide on our journey through life together.

The Mirror of Understanding: Reflecting Instead of Reacting

In the realm of heartfelt narratives, the symphony of life's orchestra plays a melody of emotions. It is within these moments that "The Mirror of Understanding: Reflecting Instead of Reacting" becomes a pivotal movement in the concerto of matrimonial communication.

Here, we learn to hold the mirror up to our own souls, reflecting on our thoughts and emotions before they manifest into the reactions that can cause ripples in the still waters of our harmony.

As partners, it is natural to encounter storms that evaluate the strength of our vessel—an offhand remark igniting a tempest of feelings, or a miscommunication steering us into a gale of misunderstanding. However, the essence of our joint journey is not found in the avoidance of such squalls, but in mastering the art of navigating through them with wisdom and grace. This mastery is born from the sacred pause—the quiet space between stimulus and response where true reflection resides.

It is within this hallowed pause that we discover the power to transform instinctive reactions into intentional responses. By peering into the mirror of understanding, we bear witness to the contours of our inner landscape—the hills of our hopes and the valleys of our fears. It is a land rich with the history of our experiences, painted with the brushstrokes of our vulnerabilities.

In this space, patience blooms like a rose in the dawn's early light, its petals unfolding with a tenderness that soothes the prickling thorns of defensiveness. Patience is the gardener that cultivates a bed of empathy, where we can lie down in the soil of each other's perspectives, nurturing the seeds of compassion until they blossom into a shared view.

When dialogue becomes a prism, refracting the light of our different truths into a spectrum of understanding, we are gifted with a vision of empathy. To empathetically reflect rather than impulsively react is to engage in a sacred communion with the spirit of our spouse. It is the gentle art of hearing not only the words said but also the unspoken language of the heart, allowing love to be both the question and the answer.

The mirror of understanding teaches us to recognize the shared humanity that binds us—flaws and imperfect beauty entwined. Here, communication transcends the barriers of ego, and in the shared reflection, we catch a glimpse of the divine essence that is mirrored in one another.

We embrace the wisdom that every reaction has a source—a tender spot that aches to be acknowledged, a longing to be seen, a memory reaching out for validation. And in this awareness, our conversations become an alchemy that transmutes the base metals of conflict into the precious gold of deeper intimacy.

With hearts open wide and souls bared to the soft light of understanding, we prepare to continue our sojourn through the sacred corridors of marital dialogue. It is here that we weave the threads of intimacy through the loom of words, crafting a tapestry of union that holds the stories of who we are, who we have been, and who we aspire to become, joined side by side, in silence and in speech.

Weaving Threads of Intimacy Through Words

In the garden where patience and empathy flourish, sotto voce, we find ourselves amidst the verdant growth of intimacy. "Weaving Threads of Intimacy Through Words" is akin to mastering the loom that binds two souls in a colorful tapestry of shared life. Each thread is a word, a phrase, a tender disclosure that, when intertwined, forms the warm blanket of our love. Words have the power to both construct and navigate the intricate passageways of the heart, to build bridges across the streams of our consciousness which, until spoken aloud, were invisible.

Let us, in this quest for closeness, acknowledge the vigor of soft-spoken truths and the gentle caress of a listening ear. It is for us to learn the language that dresses naked souls, to select with care the fabrics of our phrases, knowing each has the potential to either soothe or chafe the spirit. Communicating with intention means choosing expressions that uplift, encourage, and affirm—the kind of words that plant gardens within the soul, where peace and love can harvest.

Each conversation is a shared journey, a step closer to the beating drum of our united heart. Within this communion, active listening becomes our compass, pointing towards understanding as we navigate through the mist of assumptions and the marshes of misinterpretation. Active listening is not only about hearing but also about experiencing the world as our partner does, with all its hues and textures.

Remember, our love is a masterpiece composed of strokes both bold and delicate; within this frame, the varicolored expressions of our admiration for one another must shine forth. The whispers of "I appreciate you," the soft echoes of "I understand," and the strong, yet gentle, declarations of "I am here" serve as colors in our palette, painting a scene of connection that transcends the spoken language.

Encouraging and enacting these verbalizations demands the courage to be both expressive and receptive, to give voice to our affection, and to pause in the warmth of our partner's replies. It is the exchange of dialogue that dances with the rhythm of vulnerability, swaying gracefully to tunes of mutual desire for closeness and adoration.

Here we find the balance, the ebb and flow of giving and receiving, an equilibrium that is the heartbeat of a thriving relationship. The small daily deposits we make into the emotional bank account of our marriage—compliments, acknowledgments, expressions of love—these are the currencies that enrich us beyond measure.

As we continue to weave this tapestry, let us be mindful that the language we use is but an outpouring of the heart's true contents. Our narrative remains incomplete without the silent articulations of our beings: the tender touch, the shared glance, the companionable silence—all reinforcing the vibrancy of our verbal tapestry.

Having cultivated the fields of understanding and nurtured the blooms of intimacy through empathetic communication, we ready ourselves to transition gently towards exploring the symphony of love's varied expressions. From understanding to sharing to embodying love, our journey merges the seen and unseen—verbal and nonverbal—into the unity of a melody that caresses the soul. In the dance of love's dialect, we find our rhythm, majestic and endearing, ready to step into the next flow of our connection: the harmonious exchange of affection both spoken and shown.

The Language of Love: Expressing Affection Verbally and Non-Verbally

As the sacred dance of marriage unfolds, we understand that our love story is composed of more than mere words—it is a living, breathing entity that thrives on the nuanced symphony of gestures, touch, and the silent poetry of presence. In "The Language of Love: Expressing Affection Verbally and Non-Verbally," we attune our beings to the delicate frequencies of nonverbal communication, the whispers of the heart that do not traverse the vocal cords yet sing volumes through the simplest of actions.

The caress of a hand, the fondness in a gaze, or the gentle security in a shared silence—these are the wordless verses of affection that lace the air with tenderness. They remind us that affection is a river that flows from the soul, meandering through the channels of our daily interactions, nourishing the roots of our bond with the water of unspoken understanding.

This dialogue of the heart asserts itself in the small acts of kindness that stitch the hours of our days together: preparing a meal with care, a knowing smile across a crowded room, the warmth of a hug after a weary day, or walking hand in hand, side by side, as silent sentinels of a love that needs no declarations to validate its depth.

In the outcome of these expressions, we find a safe harbor for our vulnerabilities, a sanctuary where words are not the currency, yet love is abundant and overflowing. Here, the soft brush of fingertips on a cheek can say "I love you" in a language that predates speech, resonating with an emotional clarity that pierces the heart's core.

And yet, we must not lay to rest the power of the spoken word, for it, too, is a vital thread in the tapestry of our intimacy. When we voice our love, it reverberates in the sacred spaces between us, echoing through the chambers of our mutual existence, affirming, and reaffirming the truth we live by. The "I cherish you" that greets our partner's ear is a clarion call to the soul, a reminder of the treasure that they are to us, more precious than the rarest of gems.

In this intricate interplay of verbal and non-verbal language, we find the balance, the harmony that forms the bedrock of our togetherness. Like seasoned musicians, we learn when to let our actions compose the melody and when to let our words write the lyrics. It is in this synchronicity that the language of love achieves its fullest expression, an eloquent testament to the beauty of our union.

Let us carry this wisdom forward, holding it like a beacon as we venture into the affirmations that anchor our commitments to one another. With each gesture, each word, we are composing a continuous affirmation that resonates with fidelity, respect, and everlasting devotion. The language of love is not just spoken or shown; it is lived. And as we endow our life with these expressions of love, we ready ourselves for solitude.

Affirmation of Connection

"I choose to practice the generosity of assumption, always seeing the best in my partner's intentions, words, and actions. Rooted in love and respect, our bond grows stronger with every positive thought."

As we traverse the journey of married life, the heart longs for an anthem, a chorus of connection that resonates within the sacred walls of unity. "Affliction of Connection" is that anthem, a declaration of our pledge to foster an enduring bond, built on the bedrock of compassionate communication. It is a vow that we recite with every action and rekindle with every word, embedded within the echoing chambers of our collective heart.

Here, let us pause and gather the wisdom harvested from our shared narratives, to compose a covenant of enduring love and mutual respect. We stand under the canopy of trust we have woven with threads of understanding, emboldened to express the resolute affection that seals our allegiance to one another. With hands clasped and gazes intertwined, we affirm:

"I am yours, in the joyful symphony and the silent sorrows. I am the listener to your spoken dreams and the silent fears that you dare not voice. I am the witness to your highest peaks and your darkest valleys. My embrace is your shelter, my heart is your home."

Let this affirmation thrum through our daily lives, an unspoken promise that echoes in the earnest effort to appreciate our partner's silent struggles and unspoken joys for in our understanding, in our active listening, and in the daily dance of our verbal and non-verbal exchange, we become artisans of a profound truth: Love, in its purest form, is an active, living testament to the grace we bestow upon one another.

As we nurture this enduring connection, the lyrical beauty of our interactions creates a melody that draws others to the warmth of our devotion. We become a beacon of hope, a testament to what it means to move through the world as harmonious custodians of sacred love.

As the sun sets on this chapter, we are ready to cross a new threshold. We move forward, holding the music of compassionate communication in our hearts, ready to step into the gentle luminescence of a deeper understanding. We embark on this voyage with the courage that comes from knowing our foundation is strong and our spirits are entwined, emboldened to explore the spiritual essence of intimacy, where love's true unity flourishes.

3

Bliss

Spirit-Filled

MK Photography

Cultivating Serenity in the
Spirit-Filled Home

PRINCIPLE: A home bathed in spirituality and love becomes a sanctuary of peace; every room echoes with harmony, and every corner is filled with bliss.

BLISS PROTOCOL #12: Spiritual Connection:

- **Scenario:** Spiritual disconnection
- **Solution:** Shared spiritual practice
- **Implementation:** Spiritual exploration
- **Key advice:** Deepen spiritual bond

Foundations of a Spirit-Filled Sanctuary

In the heart of every dwelling where love is the cornerstone and faith the keystone, there pulses an ancient rhythm—a timeless melody of serenity that dances through the halls and whispers through the walls. This is the essence of a spirit-filled sanctuary, a place where the cacophony of the world fades into sweet, harmonious silence, and the soul, unburdened, can soar.

In these sacred enclaves, we find more than a mere residence; we discover a refuge crafted by our own hands and hearts—a testament to the divine tapestry that is family life. Here, within these spirit-bathed rooms, harmony reigns, and the troubles that besiege us from the outside world lose their power, disarmed by the vibrant shield of unity and purpose that we, as couples and families, weave each day.

Lachele's account of their lived experience draws us into the profound meaning of such a sanctuary. When tempests howl and trials thunder at our door, it's the spiritual foundation within our homes that serves as our bulwark, allowing peace to dwell amidst the storms.

It's the daily rituals of prayer, forgiveness, patience, understanding, and unyielding love that fortify the walls of our domestic haven. It's the divine principles, deeply embedded in every corner, every shared meal, every embrace, which make our homes true sanctuaries of the spirit.

This foundation is a conscious choice, a mutual covenant between husband and wife—an agreement that, no matter the interference of children, careers, or financial strains, their home will remain a steadfast oasis of spiritual tranquility. Through this steadfast commitment, we send an invincible message to the world and ourselves: Our domestic sanctum is unassailable, for it is built upon the unconditional love and divine wisdom that binds us together.

As we embark on this journey through the chapters that follow, we explore the myriad ways in which we can enshrine these principles into the very essence of our living spaces, transforming our daily lives into spiritual odysseys. With every step, we walk the path toward a more profound connection, a more compassionate understanding, and a more enriching union with each other and the divine.

The promise of this chapter to you, dear reader, is that of a blueprint—a guiding light to constructing a home that not only shelters but also rejuvenates the spirit. We will delve deep into strategies that bridge spirituality with the practicalities of domestic life. We will share stories of compromise, empathy, and the sweet alchemy of peaceful coexistence. We will offer insights on designing a home that doubles as a spiritual sanctuary, reflective of the values you hold dear.

Together, we will understand the symphony of home harmony, manifested through rituals and traditions that invigorate and unite. And finally, we will compose an affirmation—your family's unique declaration of serenity and commitment to this spirit-filled life.

So let us begin with intention, love, and open hearts, willing to learn and eager to transform, as we move toward manifesting the very essence of domestic bliss—a home harmonizing in the profound serenity of the spirit.

Growing Serenity in the Spirit-Filled Home

The Balancing Act of Spirituality and Domesticity

Every abode, much like a sacred tabernacle, has within it the potential to nurture the spirit, to become a sanctuary where divine presence and daily routine dance in syncopated harmony. This equilibrium, where the tangible meets the ethereal, where earthly chores align seamlessly with celestial whispers, is the art and science of balancing spirituality with domesticity.

The pilgrimage towards striking this balance begins not outside our thresholds, but within the confines of our own hearts and homes. It is a delicate waltz between the sacred and the everyday—a waltz that Kofie and Lachele have mastered throughout their marriage. Their story invites us into an intimate alcove, displaying the quiet elegance of aligning spiritual practice with the hum of domestic life.

Kofie recalls, with a sparkle reminiscent of the twilight's first star, the momentous task of marrying their distinctive spiritual upbringings. His roots, deeply watered by the Methodist traditions, sought sunlight alongside Lachele's blossoms, tended in the Baptist faith. As their lives intertwined, they fashioned a shared spiritual climate, a greenhouse where love, rather than dogma, cultivated the rarest of blooms.

Through this intertwined spirituality came the necessary melding of their worlds—not only of faith but of the demands of their careers and personal aspirations. Kofie's landscape of creativity, shaped by the scissors and combs of the hair industry, found a kindred spirit in Lachele's disciplined terrain, marked by the rhythm of law enforcement. Together, they navigated a domesticity punctuated by schedules, finances, and dreams, each thread woven into a tapestry of shared purpose and progress.

The strategies that guided them, the principles etched into the milestones of their journey, stand as beacons to those who seek to follow in their footsteps. These strategies, akin to the keys of a grand piano, unlock the doors to rooms suffused with tranquility, to kitchens reverberating with laughter, and to bedrooms steeped in whispered prayers and dreams.

For Kofie and Lachele, the morning's first rays bring more than light; they bring a moment of communion with the divine. Their daily rituals—whether carved out before the sun's debut or beneath the evening's celestial canvas—do not exist in isolation. They are accompanied by the symphony of preparing meals, attending to the children's laughter and tears, and a myriad of other quotidian melodies.

Such synchrony between the sacred and the daily does not occur by chance. It is the product of intention, a deliberate weaving of prayer, meditation, and reflection into the fabric of their lives. It requires the setting aside of moments—sacred pauses—in which the soul can drink deeply from the wellspring of spirituality and emerge renewed to face the tasks at hand.

Yet, even as we bask in the light of this balance between the spiritual and the mundane, we are naturally drawn to the heartbeats of those who share our spaces, our lives. The joining of souls in the familial bond is a tapestry rich with diverse threads—each adding complexity, beauty, and depth. It is these connections, the ways in which we welcome new threads into our tapestry, which beckon us further along this journey of domestic bliss.

This, then, is the invitation extended: to see in Kofie and Lachele's story a reflection of our own potential. May their walk inspire us to find, within our own lives, the rhythm that unites spirituality with the everyday—the rhythm that allows us to craft a home not just of walls and windows, but one of hearts and hymns, a dwelling that truly is a refuge of serenity. Let us now turn our gaze to these sacred bonds, to the merging of families and spirits, and discover the alchemy that transforms a collection of individuals into a tapestry woven with the golden threads of love and togetherness.

Weaving New Threads into the Family Tapestry

The Art of Embracing Wholeness

Within the walls of a home where love is the language and understanding the currency, the weaving of new threads into the family tapestry is an art form of the highest order. In the sacred journey of marriage, nothing stands still; life breathes into each day new beginnings, new challenges, and fresh faces to love and understand.

As we nurture our spirit-filled sanctuary with intention and grace, we must also turn our hearts to embrace the ever-evolving nature of family. With every new soul that crosses our threshold, we are given a fresh spool of thread to incorporate into our tapestry, an opportunity to enrich the fabric of our collective lives with vibrant, new hues.

This is a dance of love, delicate and profound, as we open our arms to children who may come into our lives by birth, marriage, or providence. Each child, each new family member, is a note added to the marital symphony—a note that holds the power to change the tempo, to introduce a new melody, and to harmonize the existing chorus in unforeseen, yet beautiful ways.

The blending of lives and traditions is not without its complexities. It demands of us an unwavering commitment to patience and empathy, as we learn the contours of each other's hearts and stories. Like Kofie and Lachele, who have tenderly unfolded each layer of their joined experiences, we too must learn to celebrate the richness that differing backgrounds and cultures present.

Imagine the dining room table, an altar of sorts, where shared meals become sacred rituals. Here, a feast of not just food, but tales and laughter, creates an alchemy that transforms individuals into a united whole. This is the joyous culmination of allowing love to lead the way—of affirming that every member, new or longstanding, is an integral strand in the family tapestry.

Through this induction of new threads, we find our family stories expanding. These are the stories that reflect not just a single journey, but a compendium of journeys, woven side by side, each distinct yet joining to form a more beautiful whole. It is these threads that build the sheltering tapestry, offering warmth, comfort, and the deep-seated sense of belonging we all yearn for.

Yet, the incorporation of these new threads requires more than passive acknowledgment—it demands active engagement with the practices that cultivate acceptance, understanding, and celebration. Language, traditions, and values—each must be considered and interlaced with the utmost care. The process is akin to the crafting of a quilt, with each square representing a cherished memory, belief, or hope, carefully pieced together in a labor of love.

Thus, as we traverse this dimension of our relational odyssey, our homes should radiate the warmth of our willingness to grow and adapt. Fostering an environment that is inclusive, where each voice is heard and each uniqueness is treasured, is the essence of building a thriving, spirit-filled home.

Yet, the work does not stop by simply welcoming new members. It continues as we learn the art of peaceful coexistence, of harmonizing our daily interactions to ensure that our home remains a bastion of serenity, even in the middle of a rich tapestry of our collective existence. Let us gently turn the page and delve into the wisdom of managing the inevitable ebbs and flows that come with domestic life, embracing the alchemy that maintains joy and tranquility at the core of our spirit-filled homes.

The Alchemy of Peaceful Coexistence

The Harmony of Hearts and Habitation

Within the spirit-filled home lies a profound alchemy, an ability to transmute the leaden weights of daily friction into the golden moments of peaceful coexistence. Just as a silken web is not woven by a single thread, so too is the serenity within our homes crafted by the countless intertwining strands of understanding, compassion, and respect.

Imagine the home as a crucible in which the fires of passion, ambition, and individuality are melded to create something far more enduring: a family united not merely by blood or law, but by the shared commitment to harmony in the midst of life's inevitable dissonances.

As guardians of this domestic tranquility, we must cultivate the garden of our relationships with the diligence of an expert horticulturist. Each interaction, from the most mundane exchange to the most heated discussion, presents an opportunity to seed empathy and weed out discord. By anchoring ourselves in the values we hold dear—patience, kindness, and a willingness to listen—we construct a foundation strong enough to weather any storm.

Consider the times when voices rise like a tempest, where differing points of view clash like thunder. These are not the harbingers of chaos, but rather, the natural rhythms of a home alive with the passions of its inhabitants. In these storms, our strength as a couple is evaluated, but it is also tempered—honed into a force capable of bending without breaking.

Among these tempests, we find solace in retreating to our personal sanctuaries, quiet spaces within our home where we can reflect and reconnect with our inner compass. These sacred pauses are not admissions of defeat, but strategic withdrawals that allow us to return to the fray equipped with greater wisdom and clarity.

And so, we learn to navigate the tides of coexistence by paddling in unison, choreographing our movements to the rhythm of mutual respect and shared vision. Conflict resolution becomes less a battle to be won and more a dance to be performed, a balancing act between assertiveness and acquiescence, ensuring that the tapestry of our family life remains vibrant and intact.

It is viscerally understood, within these walls that resonate with laughter and whispers and sometimes tears, that compromise is not capitulation but the alchemy through which love transfigures personal desire into collective joy.

This is the legacy we bestow upon children and all who enter our sanctuary: the lesson that peace is not found in the absence of conflict, but in the beauty of its resolution. With each resolution, the bonds of our family are reinforced, becoming conduits of unwavering support and unspoken understandings.

Let us then cross the threshold into the next endeavor with tranquil hearts, as we seek to mirror the inner peace of our spirits in the physical realm of our abode. From the design of reflective spaces to the tangibility of meditation corners, we stand at the precipice of creation, ready to delve into the sacred task of aligning our home's physicality with the spiritual vibrancy we have cultivated. Being intentional in design invites a flowing transition into the kingdom of sacred spaces, where every corner, every nook of our dwelling becomes an extension of the ethereal sanctuary we tirelessly nurture within.

Sacred Spaces: Creating Physical and Spiritual Harmony

The Architecture of Soulful Dwellings

As we stand within the heart of our abode, cradled by the love and peace we've nurtured, our spirits yearn for a physical manifestation of the tranquility we cherish. This is the threshold upon which we embark on creating sacred spaces, havens within our homes that resonate with the timbre of our spiritual longings and the essence of our shared dreams.

Sacred spaces serve as a testament to the spiritual foundation we've set forth, a visible embodiment of our inner sanctuaries where we can retreat, reflect, and connect. Just as the roots of a time-honored oak tree delve deep into the earth, these physical spaces anchor us, providing a touchstone for our souls amid the ebbs and flows of life's complexities.

In the artistry of our home's design, we embed the melodies of calm and concentration, crafting corners dedicated to meditation, walls that whisper heritage, and rooms that echo with mantras of love. Each space becomes a canvas upon which we paint our values, a gallery of our collective hearts' aspirations.

Consider the reading nook, with shelves brimming with wisdom, where each book is a friend, each paragraph a conversation with ancestors and guides. Envision the meditation corner, its cushions imbued with the scent of sandalwood, where silence becomes the language through which we commune with the divine.

The importance of this endeavor invokes a sacred duty within us, lighting the path through the intricate dance of decoration and symbolism. We adorn these spaces with items that speak to our journey: vibrant tapestries that carry the legacy of our heritage, candles that flicker with the promises we've made, and photographs that chronicle the footsteps we've taken together.

As architects of a spiritually harmonious home, we bridge the tangible with the ethereal, constructing altars of remembrance and promise. Here, the simple act of lighting a candle becomes a rite, transforming the mundane into the mystical, and inviting an aura of serenity to envelop our shared experiences.

We take to heart the creed that every space within our walls should bear witness to the laughter, the struggles, and the quiet victories of our union. The dining area, where we break bread, stands as a sanctuary for gratitude and sustenance, and the backyard blooms as a testament to the vivacity of our love and the nurturing hands that tend it.

By infusing our dwelling with holistic design, we honor not just our personal faith, but the collective spirit that lifts our family heavenward. Therein lies the power to elevate everyday interactions into transformative experiences, turning the key to unlocking the deepest wellsprings of harmony in our daily lives.

From the kitchen where we blend spices and stories, to the bedroom where dreams are enfolded in the embrace of rest, no corner is left untouched by our intention. Each step we take within these halls should carry the feather-light touch of the sacred, brushing our days with the dew of spiritual presence.

As we cultivate these sacred spaces, we weave a ribbon of silent prayer into the very fabric of our existence, entwining our breath with the heartbeat of home. It is within these hallowed grounds that we look to kindle the flames of home harmony, inviting rituals and traditions to ignite our collective joy and bind us ever closer. Let us then glide gracefully into the embrace of these rituals, carrying with us the spirit of unity that pervades every sacred space we have lovingly curated.

The Symphony of Home Harmony

Rhythms and Rituals That Resonate

In the sacred spaces we've tenderly cultivated, let us now breathe life into the symphony of our domestic harmony, where carefully chosen rituals and cherished traditions become our shared song. In the intricate dance of day-to-day life within our spirit-filled homes, it is the rituals we embrace and the traditions we uphold that form the melodious backbone of our familial experience.

Here, within the hallowed confines of hearth and heart, we craft a cadence that keeps time with our highest aspirations. The morning ritual of sharing affirmations over breakfast, the chorus of laughter filling the room as stories are shared, these are more than mere moments—they are the beats per measure in our marriage's masterpiece.

With intention, we set the week's rhythm with Sunday suppers, a homage to the legacy of kinship and the resonance of gratitude. The table becomes our altar, laden with dishes seasoned with history and garnished with hope, a feast where every bite is infused with the flavors of our collective journey.

Gathered around this table, we share the sustenance of spirited conversations, a communion that fortifies both body and soul. As we break bread, our shared narratives splice into the tapestry of generational wisdom, each thread vital to the vibrancy of the tapestry we weave together.

And in these communal moments, eyes meet, and hands join in unison that surpasses the confines of our sanctuary, reaching back through the annals of our rich heritage. We honor those who came before us, whose strength and sacrifices set the stage for the melodies we now compose with tender reverence.

Celebrations become crescendos bursting with jubilation at the milestones reached, with the gathering of loved ones serving as a testament to the enduring harmony that marriage and commitment foster. Birthdays, anniversaries, and accolades—all merit a chorus of acknowledgment in our household's nurturing oasis.

Each spouse, and each child is allotted a solo—time to shine, to be seen and heard in their authenticity. From the show-and-tells of treasured possessions to the spotlight of individual achievements, these solo pieces infuse the symphony with texture and depth, a cacophony of voices harmonizing in a family's unconditional love.

In the quiet night, as the moon stands as the conductor's baton, we engage in the nightly tradition of reflection. In each other's embrace, the worries of the world dissipate, replaced by a serenity that envelops our sacred cocoon, a promise whispered through kisses goodnight.

Our rituals, diverse as the shades of our skin, reflect the spectrum of our shared life, each practicing a tone in the melody of our union. With each tradition upheld, we build the repertoire of our home's symphony, composing a score that will echo throughout the chambers of tomorrow.

As the notes of one ritual fade into silence, we pivot deftly into the spaces of introspection and resolve, into the rhythms of affirmation and serenity. Here, we distill the essence of our journey, a chord progression that leads us from the vibrancy of our rituals to the tranquil repose of reflection and promise for tomorrow.

BLISS: Cultivating Serenity in the Spirit-Filled Home

In the Echoes of Rituals, A Promise Kept

Affirmation: *"Through shared practices, meaningful conversations, and acts of service and compassion, we deepen our spiritual connection, fostering a bond that transcends challenges and brings us closer to divine harmony."*

As the final notes of our symphony of home harmony linger in the air, carrying with them the laughter and wisdom of our familial concord, we settle into the introspective cadence of serenity. This is where reflection and affirmation entwine, offering us the chance to weave the delicate shawl of peace around our shoulders and affirm the promises made within the spirit-filled sanctuary we call home.

In this sanctified retreat of our collective soul, we understand that serenity is not merely an absence of discord, but the presence of peace— a peace that is cultivated with each gentle word, each deed steeped in love, and each moment of shared silence. Our affirmation, both spoken and unspoken, is the trellis upon which the blossoms of tranquility grow.

In our hearts, where the warmth of commitment smolders, we rekindle the vow to protect, to nurture, and to honor the oasis we have co-created. We affirm the resilience we possess, a heritage inherited from ancestors who whispered prayers into the winds and mastered the art of turning trials into triumphs with a song in their hearts.

We declare, with the tenderness of a lover's touch and the fortitude of a warrior's resolve, that we will continue to uphold the customs that bind us, transcending the mundane to touch the divine. Our sanctuary shall remain a place where every child knows their worth, where every elder's story is revered, where every hardship is met with joined hands and unwavering faith.

It is here, in the quiet stillness, that we speak our affirmation of serenity:

"May our home always be a harbor in the tumultuous sea of life, a space where peace reigns supreme, grounded in the bedrock of spiritual tenacity.

May our love be a beacon that shines forth, guiding us through the fog of the unknown, and reminding us that, together, we are the lighthouse standing tall against the night."

With each dawn, as the sun stretches its golden fingers across our threshold, we embrace the day with the calm assurance that our serenity springs eternal from the depths of our devotion. Each meal shared, each prayer whispered, and each challenge faced with grace is another stitch in the quilt of our serene existence.

Our home's sanctuary pulses with a rhythm only the heart can understand, a rhythm that beckons us to join in the dance of living fully, loving deeply, and leading with the lantern of spirit-filled bliss. It is within this dance that we find solace and strength, the confluence of the sacred and the everyday.

As the day departs and the stars emerge to share their ancient wisdom with the world below, we nestle into the embrace of the night, carrying with us the affirmations that echo through our spirits. They follow us into the realm of dreams, promises cradled in the arms of the midnight hour.

And when the morrow winks its first eye, a new canvas awaits us, an unwritten chapter ready to be graced by the brush of our continuous journey. Here, at the threshold of tomorrow, we hold true to our ethos of resilience, love, and unity. With hearts brimming with anticipation and renewed purpose, we step boldly into the dawning light, ready to redefine the flex, the give and take, that comes with the beautiful ebb and flow of *"That Marriage Lyfe."*

4

The Art of Constructive Conflict

Constructive Conflict

Bethune Graphics

Transforming Disputes into Bridges of Understanding

PRINCIPLE: *"Conflict, when navigated with love and respect, becomes a canvas for growth and deeper connection."*

BLISS PROTOCOL #13: Healthy Conflict, Deeper Understanding:

- **Scenario:** Destructive conflict patterns
- **Solution:** Constructive disagreement
- **Implementation:** Conflict resolution
- **Key advice:** Use conflict for growth

In the crucible of our closest relationships, particularly the sacred union of marriage, we encounter the raw materials of our character, refined, and shaped by the fires of conflict. As we journey together through this chapter, let us reframe the way we perceive discord—not as an insurmountable rift but as a forge for the strongest of bonds.

Within these pages, we speak a truth that resonates with the rhythm of transformation: that conflict, when navigated with love and respect, becomes a canvas for growth and deeper connection (Principle).

This is not the jarring clatter of armor and swords but the harmonious clinking of the sculptor's tools—each disagreement, each misunderstood word, an opportunity to sculpt a masterpiece of deeper understanding and intimacy. Imagine, if you will, a canvas stretching before you, blank and laden with possibility.

Now envision each stroke of conflict as a sway of the brush, its bristles laden with the vibrant colors of emotions, thoughts, and dreams. With every touch against the canvas, a shared story unfolds—a portrait of struggle, resilience, and transformative beauty.

Our avatar walks the path of resilience and richness, deeply rooted in the African American experience. Through the triumphs and trials of matrimony, they seek harmony, drawing from cultural wellsprings of communication, spiritual growth, and emotional nurturing. They carry the legacy of love, threading the rich tapestry of their heritage into every aspect of their union, while navigating the nuances of building family, fostering connectivity, and achieving collective growth.

The aim of "That Marriage Lyfe" is to serve as a beacon, casting a light that guides couples through the tempestuous waters of marital life, steering them towards shores of wisdom, grace, and authenticity. Here, we embark on a journey to stoke the embers of joy and intimacy within marriages, to buff the link of understanding until it gleams, and to buttress the familial stronghold—brick by spiritual brick—upon the foundations laid down by those who walked the road before us.

Let us not shy away from the profundities of marriage, the poetics of partnership. In the melodious tone inspired by the likes of Maya Angelou and the fervor of T.D. Jakes, we wrap our prose in a tapestry that comforts and challenges, which holds and releases, that dances with the cadence of an eternal love song.

We weave through this narrative an invitation to see, in each other, both the mirror and the light—the reflection of our own selves and the illumination of our better angels.

In this first section, as we tenderly unwrap the layers of "Embracing Conflict as Opportunity," we will uncover the golden threads that can sew together torn seams and patchwork disagreements with the artistry of understanding and compassion. You will learn not merely to traverse the battlefield of differing opinions but to walk hand in hand across bridges of understanding that span the emotional divides.

It is a promise—a covenant of sorts—that by embracing the teachings within, you will find new strength in vulnerability, new resonance in your shared voices, and a refreshed commitment to the unity that thrives through the tempest. Together, we will paint with broad strokes of heart and spirit, crafting a narrative that not only acknowledges the challenges of confrontation but cherishes the revelatory moments that follow.

As this section draws to a close, anticipate the unfolding story, a passage from shadows into light, from discord to symphonic peace. Feel the threads of anticipation, of hope. Carry with you the principle that rests at the heart of our journey: that within the crucible of conflict lies the transformative alchemy that will lead to an unbreakable union, richer in its depth, enduring in its legacy.

Breaking the Cycle of Repetitive Arguments

The Haunting Echoes of Past Discord

Sitting across from one another, hands clasped amidst the echoes of a dispute that feels like an age-old record on repeat, we find ourselves ensnared in a tangle of words and emotions, replaying the same arguments. It's a cycle that can leave our hearts weary and our union fractured by the weight of unresolved sentiments—a cycle that demands our attention if we are to pave the way to a relationship brimming with understanding and peace.

Recognizing the Melody of Misunderstanding

To break this cycle, we must first attune our ears to the melody of misunderstanding that plays beneath the surface of our quarrels. Is it a note of unfulfilled expectations, a harmony of unmet needs, or a rhythm of fears unvoiced? By tracing the origin of this familiar tune, we begin to grasp the deeper issues that fuel our repetitive episodes and root our conflicts in the fragile soil of uncertainty.

Harmonizing Heart and Mind

The true artistry of solving these recurring disagreements is in harmonizing the heart and the mind. It calls for a delicate balance, a willingness to listen with an open spirit and respond with a clarity that transcends mere retort. Ground your conversations in a shared commitment to uncover the issues that trigger these cycles.

Converse with the candor of soulmates and the wisdom of those who have walked the path of love and stumbled—only to rise again, stronger, and more united.

The Dance of Dialog and Discovery

Embark on a journey together where each step is a move towards mutual understanding and resolution. Embrace the dance of dialogue and discovery, turning each conflict into a choreographed sequence that leads to the heart of the matter.

As we peel away the layers of discord, we find at the core the raw, unvarnished truth that seeks acknowledgment—not as indictments but as signposts pointing us toward the healing we both crave.

Crafting a New Narrative

Let us then craft a new narrative, a story handwritten of patience and the ink of introspection. Replace the tired script of blame and confrontation with words that uplift, support, and cherish. For in this new dialogue, we do not speak just to be heard, but to forge an understanding that resonates with the depths of our shared experiences.

Echoing Through the Halls of Change

As this journey from echoing disputes to constructive conversation unfolds, the walls that once echoed with strife reverberate now with sounds of breakthrough and renewal. We seize the opportunity to infuse our connection with newfound strength, transforming the relentless noise of contention into a whisper of profound recognition—the harmonious sound of two hearts in tune.

Sustaining the Symphony of Solutions

In the delicate art of turning discord into harmony, let us also be mindful to sustain the symphony of solutions that we create. Building upon each resolution, fortify the bonds that unite us, and set in motion a rhythm of love and understanding that can endure the tests of time.

With the wisdom of silencing the clamor of past patterns, we gingerly step into a realm of love that thrives in the sunlight of open, honest, and nurturing communication. Here in this space, we discover the undercurrent of faith that carries us forward, ever drawing us closer to the sacred shores of togetherness and shared spirituality.

Keeping Faith Amid Disagreement

The Sacred Harmony Within

In the sanctuary of marriage, the walls hum with whispers of unity and the echoes of discord alike. When disagreements cast a shadow over our communion, it is faith—the unwavering belief in something greater than ourselves—that illuminates our path. Holding fast to this light, even in the throes of conflict, becomes a testament to the endurance of a bond that is both human and divine.

Anchoring in Spiritual Solidarity

Amidst the storm of contention, it is the anchor of spiritual solidarity that steadies our hearts. By re-centering our perspective on the shared values that brought us together, we rekindle a sense of purpose that transcends the superficiality of the dispute.

Together, we invoke the power of prayer, meditation, or quiet reflection—sacred practices that serve as bridges over troubled waters, reconnecting us with a collective source of strength.

The Covenant of Collective Journey

Our marriage is a covenant, a precious agreement that we honor not just in times of joy but also through the tempest of contradiction. It is a promise to uphold our vows, to see in each other the embodiment of our faith, and to navigate through disagreement with the same devotion with which we embrace our shared spirituality. This collective journey propels us forward, hand in hand, with the resilience born of belief.

The Tapestry of Trials and Triumphs

With each challenge, the tapestry of our life together grows richer, interwoven with threads of trials and triumphs. Disagreements become not merely obstacles but opportunities to demonstrate the depth of our faith in each other and the strength of our commitment to our journey. It is in the weaving of this tapestry that we find the beauty of our union, each strand a story of overcoming and each color a shade of understanding.

Reframing Dissonance into Melodies of Growth

As we navigate the sometimes-discordant waters of disagreement, we are called to reframe the dissonance into melodies of growth. By synchronizing our hearts to the rhythm of resilience, we transform the cacophony of clashing views into a concert of collaborative resolution. It is in this space of earnest seeking that we blend our voices into a chorus of solidarity, singing praises to the power of united purpose.

The Pillars of Patience and Presence

In the storied halls of such sacred unions, patience becomes the pillar upon which we lean, and presence the ground on which we stand. We learn to listen not with the intent to reply but to understand, to see through the veils of momentary emotions to the enduring spirit beneath. It is in this practice of patience and presence that the seeds of enduring love are nurtured, watered by the acknowledgment of our shared humanity.

Encircling Waves of Grace

Beyond the horizon of each contention lies the promise of renewed peace. As we tread this path, the waves of grace encircle us, reminding us that the essence of our unity is not found in the absence of conflict but in the ways we rise above it. Embracing this truth, we find ourselves enveloped in an embrace that heals, an understanding that empowers, and a love that fortifies.

In this sacred space of togetherness, let us remember that while the road through disagreement is fraught with challenges, it is a journey that deepens our connection and refines our love. With each step taken in faith, each lesson learned from the heart, we prepare ourselves for the ongoing voyage. The foundation rebuilt through faith now provides the strength to approach future challenges not as insurmountable barriers but as gateways to a more profound intimacy and trust, a prelude to the continued evolution of our relationship.

Rebuilding Trust and Intimacy Post-Conflict

The Healing Embrace

In the tender aftermath of discord, where the echoes of our disagreements begin to fade, lies the sacred ground for building anew. Here, in this hushed sanctuary of renewal, we find the courage to rebuild the delicate tapestry of trust with gentle hands and hearts open wide to the whispers of intimacy's return.

The Restoration of a Covenant

To restore the fabric torn by strife, we must draw from the wellspring of mutual understanding, compassion, and the renewed promise of a covenant, woven with strands of resilience. It is a process akin to mending delicate lace, each thread reconnected with the utmost care, affirming the unyielding strength found within our united spirit.

The Garden of Forgiveness

In this season of healing, we cultivate a garden where forgiveness takes root in rich soil, nurtured by the quiet rainfall of empathy and the sunlight of patient dialogue. Here, in the embrace of this garden, the seeds of trust blossom anew, releasing the fragrance of a love that is ever-evolving, forever flourishing in the wake of reconciliation.

The Dance of Reconnection

Rebuilding intimacy is akin to relearning the steps to a dance we once swayed to with effortless grace. It is in the meeting of each other's gaze, the gentle clasp of hands, and the tender surrender to the music of vulnerability, that we rediscover the rhythm of deep connection that unites our souls.

A Quiet Tapestry of Shared Experiences

With the patience of the weaver who knows each subtle nuance of the loom, we intertwine the threads of our experiences, shared and singular. Through the delicate interplay of give and take, speak and listen, hold and release, we craft a quiet tapestry that celebrates the rich complexity of our lives joined as one.

The Sustenance of Open Communication

To nourish the roots of our reborn trust, we must partake in the sustenance of open communication—a feast where words are served with intention, and every gesture resonates with meaning. We dine on the honesty that sustains us, the understanding that enriches us, and the attentive listening that fulfills us.

The Silken Bonds of Renewed Intimacy

In the soft glow of forgiveness, we wrap ourselves in the silken bonds of renewed intimacy. This is not the fragile silk spun in the naiveté of new love, but the fortified threads of a love that has weathered storms and emerged with an iridescent sheen—even more precious for the trials it has transcended.

Encircled by the magnificence of this patchwork quilt of emotion and experience, we lean into the future with a newfound assurance that the trust and intimacy we have cultivated are the cornerstones of our collective journey. With each step of faith and every act of compassion, we pave the way for a bond that is not easily shaken.

As we walk hand in hand, guided by the beacon of our shared experience, our path carries us toward the steady light of self-discovery. In the distance, the faint outline of new horizons beckons, where the tools and techniques we have gathered will serve as a compass.

This compass is directing us towards horizons of understanding and horizons where the realm of respectful and constructive conflict awaits our arrival.

The Art of Constructive Conflict
Transforming Disputes into Bridges of Understanding

The Whisper of Mutual Respect

In the quiet aftermath of restoring trust and intimacy, we find ourselves entering a space where the true artistry of constructive conflict begins to emerge. This quietude is not the absence of noise, but the presence of a deep mutual respect that allows us to navigate the ebb and flow of differing viewpoints with grace.

The Canvas of Conflict

Viewing conflict as a blank canvas offers us the opportunity to paint an exquisite picture of resolution and understanding. With each brushstroke of active listening, we allow our partner's words to color the space between us, creating a vivid mural that celebrates the diversity of our experiences.

The Sculpting of Solutions

As sculptors of compromise, we chisel away at the rigid stone of disagreement. With tools of empathy and openness, we reveal the hidden contours of a mutually satisfying resolution, observing the issue from all angles to create a form that is pleasing to both parties.

Harmony Amid Discord

Even in discord, harmony can be found when both partners tune into the same frequency of intent. In the willingness to understand before being understood, we compose a symphony of solutions that turns cacophony into a melodious concord.

The Quilt of Compassionate Communication

Through the quilt of compassionate communication, we sew patches of patience, kindness, and authenticity, enveloping each other in warmth. Each square tells a story, each stitch a promise of continued commitment to nurturing the bond we share.

Eloquent Echoes of Empowerment

In the dance of dialogue, our words become eloquent echoes that empower one another. Here, we do not speak over each other, but instead, we create a chorus that lifts both voices in a crescendo of collaboration and understanding.

The Fertile Grounds of Growth

Conflict, when approached constructively, becomes the fertile ground from which new levels of understanding and closeness grow. As gardeners of our relationship, we plant seeds of constructive disagreement, watering them with respect and cultivating them with a commitment to growth.

Carrying the Torch of Transformation

Transformation lies within our reach when we approach every dispute as an opportunity to build stronger bridges of understanding. As we navigate this terrain, we find the tools we need to foster an environment of love and forgiveness, setting the stage where rituals of reparation affirm the power of our union.

With a spirit feathered by wisdom from the experiences we have weathered together, we are called to gather under the canopy of affection, becoming artisans of amends. Here, within the sanctity of our shared commitment, we explore the profound practices that renew and celebrate our connection.

It is in this space that we learn to master the delicate alchemy of turning hurt into healing, discord into harmony, and every fracture into the solid ground upon which our love is built, all in preparation for creating a legacy of love that outshines the shadows of our past disagreements.

Love and Forgiveness
Rituals of Reconciliation

The Sacred Dance of Restoration

In the soulful tapestry of matrimony, forgiveness and love are the melodies that guide us through the rhythm of life, the hallowed tunes that bind us closer with every beat. As we advance beyond the art of constructive conflict, we wade deeper into the river of reconciliation, where every step taken is a dance of devotion, a testament to the enduring power of our bond.

The Embrace of Divine Forgiveness

In the realm where love meets forgiveness, there exists a profound serenity, a peace that surpasses the tempest of heartache. Here, we wrap our spirits in the embrace of divine forgiveness, allowing its gentle caress to heal the wounds of yesteryears and soothe the scars of misunderstandings.

Creating Sanctuaries of Solace

Our journey together summons us to create sanctuaries of solace where love can blossom uninhibited. Within these sacred spaces, we craft rituals—simple yet powerful acts of affection and forgiveness—that become the touchstones of our unity. In the same spirit, we renew vows whispered in the silent language of the heart, pledges of fidelity not just to one another but to the journey we share.

The Resurrection of Love

Each act of restitution serves as a gentle resurrection of love, a revival of the passions that first ignited the chalice of our union. It is in these thoughtful gestures—be it a tender word, a knowing glance, or a shared quietude—that we acknowledge the resilience of our affection, the kind that triumphs over trials and tribulations.

The Continuum of Compassion

Compassion, that ever-abundant wellspring, becomes a river that we channel towards one another, carving pathways to deeper understanding. We stand hand in hand, drawing from the infinite reservoir of empathy, quenching each other's thirst for acceptance and validation, reinforcing the bond that fortifies us.

The Symphony of Sincere Apologies

In this odyssey of togetherness, we bespeak sincere apologies, notes that compose a symphony of penitence and atonement. With each uttered "I'm sorry," we release the dissonance of discord, allowing harmonies of forgiveness to resonate within the halls of our shared history.

The Continuity of Connection

As we weave through the intricacies of life's dance, hand in hand with our beloved, we are reminded that connection is not a momentary thread but a continuity. It stretches beyond the horizon of the present, linking our pasts and futures in an eternal embrace.

The Threshold of a New Dawn

Standing at the threshold of a new dawn, inspired by love's limitless potential, we are called to affirm the resilience within. With each sunrise, we honor the growth we've fostered, the seeds of understanding we've sown in the garden of our relationship.

It is here, in the tender light of a new day, that we hold space for one another, basking in the love that brings forth the full bloom of our spirits.

Each day, presented anew, is an opportunity to paint our canvases with the colors of forgiveness, to erect monuments of compassion, and to compose our love story with the tenacity of hope. As we embrace the beauty of what lies ahead, we prepare to step into the next chapter, where the affirmation of resilience and growth awaits to reaffirm the unbroken circle of our shared life—rich, vibrant, and filled with the promise of experiences yet to unfold.

Affirmation of Resilience and Growth
A Testament to Our Journey Together

Affirmation: *"I embrace Love Languages 2.0, finding new and creative ways to express love and appreciation in my partner's preferred language. By going beyond the basics, we infuse our connection with vitality, care, and endless joy."*

In the sacred chorus of marital commitment, resilience and growth are the refrains that echo with each sunrise, an affirmation of love's capacity to heal and transform. Steadfast in this truth, we stand on the rich soil of shared experience, where every instance of discord has been transmuted into a steppingstone towards a more profound understanding.

The Power of Affirmations

The power of affirming one another in our shared life is akin to the warmth of sunlight coaxing a seedling from the earth. In the same way, our spoken affirmations are rays of encouragement, nurturing the blossoming of trust and affection in the garden of our relationship. Together, we affirm the strides taken, the hurdles overcome, and the sweet victories won in the quietude of our hearts.

In each other's gaze, we find resilience, the unwavering fortitude that has fortified our bond. Through trials and triumphs, our resilience has been the compass that guides us back to one another's arms, a testament to the enduring structure we've built with patience and devotion.

Cultivating Growth Through Understanding

Just as the mightiest trees are rooted in rich soil, our growth as partners is deeply embedded in the fertile ground of mutual understanding. We've learned to till this land together, sowing seeds of transparency and reaping the harvests of wisdom. With each earnest conversation, with every revelation shared, we facilitate an environment where both of us can flourish.

It is in the tenderness of understanding that we find the freedom to evolve, to unfurl the edges of our being, and extend toward new horizons. Growth, that dynamic force that propels us forward, fosters an expansiveness of spirit that serves not only our union but the legacy we leave behind.

Building Bridges of Continuous Connection

Our commitment to one another has been a sojourn of constructing bridges—spanning the widths of misinterpretation, bridging the depths of despair. These connections are lifelines, crafted with the twine of shared dreams and aspirations, and they allow us to traverse any challenge with confidence, knowing that we can reach each other, even across the turbulent seas of life.

The Symphony of Our Shared Life

Hand in hand, we compose the symphony of our shared life, each note resonating with the authenticity of our journey. In the harmonious blend of individual melodies, we find a tune that is uniquely ours, a melody that speaks of solidarity, compassion, and the unshakeable bond of companionship.

As we affix our eyes to the dawn of tomorrow, the affirmation of our growth stands as a beacon, an illuminating light that guides us through the passageways of time. It is not merely a declaration of past endurance but a vow to continue nurturing the soil of our relationship, to preserve the sanctity of our connection, and to walk hand in hand towards the peaks of our collective aspirations.

With each moment breathed in unison, we are authoring a legacy, a narrative imbued with the wisdom of lessons learned and the beauty of a romance continually rekindled. This legacy, etched into the annals of time, transcends the temporal and touches the eternal—a story of love's triumph over adversity, of spirits intertwined by an unbreakable thread of faith and perseverance.

As we tenderly close this chapter, let our hearts be light with the knowledge that what lies ahead is a path adorned with shared purpose and unified dreams. Poised at the cusp of a new chapter titled "Embracing Unified Purpose", we ready ourselves to traverse new dimensions of togetherness, synergizing our dreams into a journey woven from the same cloth of determination and grace that has brought us to this moment. Let us step forward, hand in hand, with eyes wide to the boundless potential of our shared story, ready to inscribe the pages yet to come with the indelible ink of love and legacy.

5

Unity in Intimacy

Love God, Love Me

MK Photography

Embracing the Spiritual Essence of Intimacy

PRINCIPLE "Intimacy is the soul's language of love; true unity is found when two hearts communicate beyond the physical."

BLISS PROTOCOL #5: Love Languages 2.0:

- **Scenario:** Missed expressions of love
- **Solution:** Enhanced love language practice
- **Implementation:** Creative love expression
- **Key Advice:** Expand love language fluency

In the intricate dance of matrimony, where each step is laden with the echoes of ancestral rhythms and punctuated by the beats of modernity, there rests a profound truth—a truth as old as the notion of unity itself. This truth speaks of intimacy, not merely as a physical communion but as a sacred conversation between souls. For within the sanctified chambers of love, true unity is birthed from the whispers shared beyond the flesh, where hearts connect in the hallowed space of spiritual understanding.

In the expanse of this chapter, dear kindred spirits, I invite you to embark upon a sublime odyssey. Together, we will traverse the sacred landscape of intimacy, exploring terrains where the spiritual essence of closeness wraps itself around our beings, inviting our souls to converse in a language that transcends the spoken word. It's a realm where tenderness and passion align, creating a melody that resonates with the purest depths of our collective being.

Imagine, if you will, love's symphony, where each note harmonizes with the rhythm of the heart, and every crescendo lifts us toward the heavens. This is where we journey, hand in hand, with the promise that we will emerge not just as lovers, but as soulmates sculpted from the divine essence of oneness.

In the chapters that follow, we shall peel back the layers of superficiality and delve deep to unearth the spiritual marrow of our unions. Here, we will transcend the surface to discover how our individual truths merge into a tapestry of shared existence. Through the lens of this transformative exploration, we reaffirm the powerful notion that in the sanctuary of spiritual intimacy, we encounter the most authentic version of ourselves and our beloved.

Harmonizing desires becomes an exquisite dance of give and take, a delicate ballet performed with the grace of understanding and respect. It is a dialogue where individuality and unity are not at odds but are entwined in a beautiful paradox of love.

Guided by our shared wisdom, we shall craft sacred conversations that are both cathartic and constructive, fostering a haven where vulnerability is met with warmth and respect. And within these dialogues of depth and substance, we will find the essence of togetherness.

Cultivating intimate rituals, meanwhile, offers a gateway to a shared spiritual experience—a consecrated practice that nurtures the bond and cements a legacy of affection that outlives the ephemeral.

As we venture forward, navigating conflict with compassion and understanding will emerge as an art form—a testament to our resilience and reverence for the union we steward. Here, we learn the profound truth that it is not the absence of strife but the mastery of harmonious resolution that deepens love's roots.

And finally, we will arrive at the powerful affirmation of spiritual unity, a declaration that seals our dedication to this eternal dance of togetherness. It is the culmination of our journey, yet only the beginning of a lifelong exploration of the uncharted depths of spiritual companionship.

Let us step forward, with anticipation shining in our eyes, as we prepare to embrace the full majesty of intimacy. With every word to come, may you feel inspired, empowered, and ready to weave the unseen threads of spiritual connection into the very fabric of your love.

From Surface to Soul: Deepening Spiritual Union

When we embark on the sacred journey of intimacy, we are often first captivated by the enchanting dance of physical touch—a waltz of tangible sensations that draws us magnetically to our partners. However, the essence of a profound connection lies beneath this surface, in a place where the heart and soul unite in a symphony of spiritual union. Here, we venture into the core of our being, discovering an intimacy that vibrates with the energy of shared purpose and mutual understanding.

Navigating the delicate transition from physical attraction to spiritual communion requires an unwavering commitment to the innermost self and to the spirit of one's partner. It's a pilgrimage to the soul's sanctuary, where we behold one another in our purest form, free from the veils of worldly expectation. It's an unveiling—slow, respectful, and genuine—where we honor the sanctity of our shared experiences and dreams.

To deepen this spiritual union, we must be willing to embrace vulnerability as our ally. Let us sit together in the quietude of our sacred space, sharing whispers of our deepest insecurities and loftiest aspirations. Here, we learn the profound language of the soul—a dialect expressed through gestures of kindness, words of encouragement, and the silent understanding that passes between two spirits entwined.

In this communion, we find strength in our shared faith, drawing upon the fortitude of our ancestors and the wisdom of our traditions. It is within this spiritual tapestry that we weave the threads of our lives together, crafting a bond that is robust yet supple—strong enough to weather the storms of adversity, yet flexible enough to grow and adapt through the seasons of life.

Courage, too, is a cornerstone of this journey, urging us to look beyond the ephemeral to reach the eternal. It is the courage to ask the tough questions, to seek the hidden gems within each other's souls, and to stand in our truth with an open heart. It is courage that propels us to unearth the treasures that lay buried beneath years of silent longing and unspoken dreams.

As we engage in this sacred exploration, we acknowledge that each of us is a universe unto ourselves—vast, mysterious, and brimming with untold stories. Our union becomes a celestial dance, where the gravitational pull of our individual worlds draws us closer, aligning our paths into a shared orbit of love and discovery.

And so, let us take a moment to breathe deeply, to look into the eyes of our beloved and see the reflection of our own spirit gazing back with warmth and recognition. Let this be the mirror through which we reacquaint ourselves with the essence of who we are and what we can become together unfettered by the limitations of the flesh, soaring in the boundless realm of spiritual intimacy.

As we continue this voyage, may we carry the profound awareness that intimacy is more than a physical embrace—it is a confluence of spirits, a harmonic convergence that infuses our lives with meaning and purpose. And in this awareness, we stand ready to honor not only the needs and desires that arise from our shared physicality but also those that emanate from the core of our spiritual selves.

Now, let us step forward from this foundational understanding of spiritual union and explore how we can harmonize our individual melodies into a chorus—a chorus that resonates with the intricate balance of desires and the intricate dance that enlivens both the self and the shared heartbeat of our union.

Harmonizing Desires: The Dance of Individuality and Unity

In the mosaic of marriage, each piece reflects a unique story, a singular desire etched into the essence of an individual. Yet, when these pieces are tenderly pieced together, they form a breathtaking image of unity—a testament to the harmonious balance that can be achieved. Within the sacred space of matrimony, we find ourselves engaged in a delicate ballet, a dance that respects the autonomy of the self while lovingly embracing the common ground we share with our partners.

As we attune to the rhythms of this dance, we are called to listen with the heart's ear, to understand the unspoken longings that pulse beneath the surface. We discern the gentle nudges and subtle glances that speak volumes, which call us to respond with a sensitivity that honors both our partner's individuality and the harmony of our relationship.

This is the space where love beckons us to find a common melody within the diversity of our individual tunes. We learn to choreograph our movements in a way that allows for self-expression while remaining in step with each other. It demands patience, for sometimes the rhythms may clash, and the step may falter. Nonetheless, love persists, guiding us back into the embrace where every misstep is forgiven, and every success celebrated.

Drawing from the wellspring of shared experiences, we find the inspiration to nurture the garden of desires that belong to us both. As we tend to these aspirations, we cultivate a landscape rich with the fruits of partnership—trust, support, and mutual satisfaction. It is in this garden that we witness the blooming of dreams, both shared and singular, each one receiving the sunlight of attention and the water of encouragement.

When desires are expressed, when they are met with a compassionate listening that seeks to understand rather than to judge, intimacy blossoms. It's a garden where trust is the evergreen, where vulnerability is the soil from which courage sprouts, allowing us to voice our deepest yearnings with the assurance of being heard and held in esteem.

In this union, there is strength—not the rigid strength of unbending wills, but the resilient strength of reeds swaying in the wind, rooted deeply in the soil of shared values and dreams. It is a strength that comes from the collective power of two souls journeying side by side, each supporting the other in the pursuit of their heart's true callings.

Here, we gaze upon the horizon with eyes that see beyond our own reflection, eyes that envision a future painted with the colors of our combined potential. It's a vision that acknowledges the individual desires as well as the collective aspiration, knowing that each dream, no matter how personal, adds to the magnificence of the shared tapestry.

With the understanding that these desires are not merely whims but sacred echoes of our innermost selves, we approach them with the sanctity they deserve. We approach them with the same tenderness as a musician cradling an ancient instrument, each note playing a whisper of the soul's yearning, each harmony a bridge between hearts.

So let us continue to dance, dear ones, with our individuality and our unity in a loving embrace. Let us celebrate the joy that arises when we honor the authenticity of our desires while nurturing the profound connection that we share. And as we do, may we remember that it is the interplay of give and take, the shared commitment to understanding and fulfilling our desires that turns the everyday into the extraordinary.

As we step forward, we carry the wisdom of this balance into the sacred realm of communication, where the desires of the heart are shared with both the courage of vulnerability and the compassion of understanding. It is in this space where our sacred conversations begin, where we uncover the depths of our connection, and where we find the strength to build a future together.

Sacred Conversations: Communicating About Intimacy

Within the woven tapestry of our shared existence, threads of golden communication hold the key to deeper understanding and spiritual bonding. Sacred conversations about intimacy are not merely about disclosing desires or expressing physical needs; they are about unveiling the soul, about engaging with our partner in a dance where words are both the music and the steps that guide us towards true union.

In this dialogue, hearts open like blossoms to the morning sun—vulnerable, yet eager to bask in the rays of connection. As we tread this path, we recognize the courage it takes to voice that which tremble in the unlit corridors of our hearts. Such bravery is not just admired, but held in a sacred space of mutual reverence, a sanctum where the language of intimacy transcends words, resonating at the frequency of souls in harmony.

To navigate this realm, we adopt a cadence of listening that is active, an attunement that hears beyond the spoken word and feels the deeper pulse of our partner's fears, hopes, and dreams. This is not mere conversation; this is an exchange that demands the fullness of our presence, as if each syllable carries with it the weight of our shared future. It is in this exchange that we find ourselves locking arms with vulnerability, allowing our unvarnished truths to lead us into profound connection.

Offering the stories of our yearnings without the shroud of apprehension, we build a bridge across the chasm that separateness may have carved. It is on this bridge that we find a middle ground, a sanctuary where the essence of our beings can coalesce, creating an alchemy that transforms base metals into precious connections.

In the waltz of words and silences, we learn to navigate the subtleties of undertones and the echoes of what remains unsaid. We become poets of the soul, articulating the rhythms of intimacy with a finesse that honors the sacredness of our bond. Here, within the sanctity of open-hearted discourse, we pledge to be each other's confidant, each other's mirror reflecting not just an image but the entirety of one's essence.

As we engage each other with the language of empathy, we do not flinch from the glow of scrutiny, knowing that it is only by baring ourselves to the light that we can merge fully with our partner. It is an act of mutual empowerment, whereby granting ourselves permission to be seen in our untamed beauty, we offer an invitation for our partner to do the same.

These sacred conversations are a tapestry where each thread is interlaced with respect and understanding. When woven skillfully and gently, they form a living document, a manifesto of our love, beckoning us to revisit its contents in moments of doubt or distance, reminding us of the covenant of our spiritual union.

As the threads of our discourse intertwine, creating patterns of understanding and acceptance, we prepare the fertile ground for rituals that celebrate and reinforce our bond. These rituals function as the milestones of our journey together, each one a stepping stone towards a deeper communion rooted in the shared truth and beauty of our intimate language.

Thus, our sacred conversations become the precursor to these intimate rituals, the verbal and nonverbal incantations that cast a protective circle around the sanctity of our union. They serve as the foundation upon which we build a fortress of tenderness, a haven where we can weather the storms and revel in the sunshine, ever growing closer, ever-evolving in our understanding.

Lachele's Personal Story:

When reflecting on intimacy in marriage, I'm reminded of the challenges I faced in opening up emotionally. In the early days of my marriage to my current husband, vulnerability was a struggle for me. While I trusted and deeply respected him, there was a barrier I hadn't yet identified or overcome.

My background in law enforcement had instilled in me a habit of caution, making it difficult to easily trust or show vulnerability. It was like I constantly wore my hair in a tight, professional bun, metaphorically speaking.

However, as our years together unfolded, I gradually learned to "let my hair down." My husband's own openness and vulnerability with me, coupled with his unwavering respect, created a safe space for me to lower my guards. He never pushed or forced this process, but consistently demonstrated love as described in Ephesians 5 - loving me as Christ loves the church.

This patient, respectful approach allowed me to become increasingly comfortable with vulnerability in our relationship. I discovered that when you can truly open up to your spouse, it adds a new dimension of bliss to your marriage.

The importance of effective communication and intimacy in marriage cannot be overstated. When you reach a point where you can be genuinely vulnerable with your partner, it transforms your relationship. This level of openness and trust creates a deep, fulfilling connection that enhances every aspect of married life.

Through this journey, I've learned that vulnerability, while challenging, is a crucial component of a truly blissful marriage. It's a process that requires patience, mutual respect, and consistent love - but the rewards are immeasurable.

Cultivating Intimate Rituals: Strengthening the Bond

Amid the delicate tapestry of shared lives, the act of cultivating intimate rituals becomes the loom upon which the fabric of connection is crafted. Intricately spun with the silk of spiritual beliefs and the sturdy threads of mutual values, these rituals are the daily affirmations of the soul's intertwining. They are sacred acts, prayers without words, which celebrate and fortify the union between two kindred spirits.

In the sanctuary of togetherness, these rituals manifest as gentle touchstones of presence and reverence. They may rise with dawn's light as a shared meditation, a quiet communion with each other and the Divine. They present themselves as affirmations whispered in the soft shelter of the night, a litany of love and gratitude that glimmers like moonlight on water.

These acts are conduits of connection, each one a petal in the ever-blooming lotus of intimacy. Whether it is the simple synchronicity of breathing together in stillness or the habitual grace of serving one another in small, daily deeds, each ritual resonates with the heartbeat of unity.

These practices become a rhythm, a sacred cadence that pulses through the days and seasons of a shared journey, anchoring the couple in a sea of life's capricious waves.

As these rituals unfold over time, they gather meaning the way a river collects tributaries, each moment of connection a fresh stream feeding into the vast, flowing waters of relationship. Through the giving and receiving of these intimate gestures, couples encode a language only audible to the heart, a lexicon of love that speaks in subtle inflections of empathy and understanding.

It is in the crafting of these rituals that one finds the alchemy to transform mundane moments into pearls of shared meaning. A morning kiss becomes not merely a greeting, but a renewal of vows, a testament to the devotion that thrives within the sacred space that two people have created. A shared laughter amidst the chaos of the day becomes a hymn, a sweet refrain that sings of the joy found within the fortress of their love.

These practices are not static; they evolve as the couple does, shaped and reshaped by the hands of time and experience. They breathe with the partners' growth, becoming ever more intricate and profound as each contributes to their design.

Within this evolving mural, a couple can trace the lineation of their growth, the milestones that demarcate their path, and the river forks that have guided them to the current moment of intimacy.

Cultivating such intimate rituals demands an intentional presence, a mindfulness that sees the divine in the ordinary. It requires a delicate balance, a somatic tuning that recognizes when to be still and when to move when to speak, and when to embrace the eloquence of silence.

In this shared intentionality, we uncover the courage to wade through the river of vulnerability, to peer into the depths of one another's eyes, and see there reflected the entirety of our story. In doing so, we stumble upon the power of tenderness, the gentle fortitude that enables us to hold space for each other's pain and joy in equal measure.

This tender strength fosters the ground from which conflicts can be navigated with compassion and understanding. It is within the crucible of intimate rituals that the flames of disagreements are tempered, each instance an opportunity to refine and strengthen the alloy of our bond.

As we stand at the confluence of our lives, where love's tributaries merge, we remember that growth, both individual and collective, is nurtured through these daily acts of unity. These rituals become our shared heritage, a legacy of intimacy we carry forward as we step hand in hand into the dance of life with all its undulating rhythms.

It is here that we prepare to face life's challenges unified, ready to employ the strength of our woven hearts to navigate the storms and calm seas alike.

Navigating Conflict with Compassion and Understanding

As we traverse the sacred space of matrimony, akin to any profound voyage, we inevitably encounter tempests that challenge the vessel of our union. It is amid these emotionally charged storms, where the winds of discord howl and misunderstandings thunder, that the true strength of our bond is assessed. How we navigate through these moments of conflict reveals the depth of our compassion and the resilience of our connection.

In this haven of togetherness, we acknowledge that discord is an integral part of the human experience; it is not the absence of conflict but the way we approach it that breathes life into our tapestry of unity. With each clash of perspectives, each divergence of opinion, we are presented with an opportunity to fortify our union, turning barriers into bridges that lead us back to understanding.

Engaging in disagreements with compassion requires that we first remove the armor of our egos, and that we stand unarmed with nothing but empathy in our arsenal. It is a softening of the heart, a mindful pause that allows us to see past the fog of our own convictions and glimpse the world through our partner's eyes.

When we choose to listen, truly listen, we transform conflict from a battle to be won into a symphony of deeper awareness, its dissonant chords resolving into harmonies that enrich the melody of our shared life.

Communicating through strife is akin to a delicate dance. It is knowing when to step forward with our truths, and when to step back to make room for theirs. It is the graceful pirouette of balancing speaking and listening, a rhythm set to the cadence of unconditional respect. And it is in this dance that we learn the subtle art of expressing our feelings without casting shadows on our partner's light.

As we venture through these narrowing canyons of contention, we discover that the language we use holds the power to either erect walls or open gates. Words can be the soothing balm that heals or the spark that ignites flames; thus, we choose them with the careful deliberation of a poet selecting the perfect metaphor. In doing so, we craft a dialogue that uplifts rather than undermines, and repairs the frayed edges rather than unravels the threads of our connection.

The resolution then becomes not a conquest but a communal journey, a pilgrimage towards a shared horizon. We navigate this path with the knowledge that our destination is not a place where differences are erased but one where they are embraced within the vast expanse of our love. Here, every resolution is a testament to our commitment, every reconciled disagreement, a stone laid in the foundation of our future.

In this process, we find that patience, much like the oak tree's silent growth, is a virtue needed in abundance. It grants us the foresight to recognize that healing takes time, and that forgiveness is a seed that needs tending before it can blossom into redemption. Patience teaches us to weather the storms with grace, trusting that the skies will clear, revealing once more the stars of our unity that guide us through the night.

As we emerge from the crucible of conflict, we are not fractured but forged, our love annealed in the kiln of mutual understanding. With each trial navigated, we are reminded of a simple yet profound truth: the power of love is measured not by how it thrives in quietude but by how it endures in times of adversity.

This understanding of love's resilience carves out a space of gratitude. We give thanks not only for the joyful moments that paint our memories with the hues of happiness but also for the challenges that sculpt our hearts into vessels of greater depth.

Embracing the spiritual essence of intimacy means walking hand in hand into a future where adversity is met with both courage and tenderness. In this treasured space, we prepare to affirm our spiritual unity, merging our individual melodies into a chorus that sings of a love transcendent, a bond unbroken, legacy that withstands the test of time. It is here that the next step of our journey awaits, a continuation of our shared narrative that speaks to the essence of all that we have become together.

Kofie's Personal Story:

In my experience, many couples fall into the trap of expecting their partners to understand them without explanation. This expectation often stems from the commonalities we share with our spouses, leading us to believe they can read our minds. However, what I've learned in our relationship is that assumption is a dangerous game.

It's entirely possible, and indeed common, for spouses to be unaware of each other's internal language or thought processes. This realization underscores the critical importance of clear communication about our feelings, interpretations, and the things we hold dear.

When misunderstandings occur, they can quickly escalate into arguments and contentious discussions that lead nowhere. We found ourselves caught in this cycle, like hamsters on a wheel, until we discovered powerful techniques to enhance our mutual understanding.

One key insight was recognizing why couples often resort to aggression when feeling misunderstood. We learned to transform this aggression into assertiveness, opting for direct but kind and polite communication. Instead of using accusatory phrases like "You always...", we began expressing ourselves with more nuanced language such as "Often..." or "When this happens, I feel...".

This shift in communication, coupled with our commitment to seeking what's right (guided by God's word) rather than arguing about who's right, led to a breakthrough. We found success in truly feeling heard and understood from each other's perspectives.

This journey taught us that effective communication in marriage isn't about mind-reading or assumptions. It's about having patience, being clear, and respectful in the expression of our thoughts and feelings, and a genuine effort to understand our partner's point of view. This approach has dramatically improved our relationship, fostering a deeper understanding and connection between us.

Unity in Intimacy: Embracing the Spiritual Essence of Intimacy

Affirmation: *"I embrace Love Languages 2.0, finding new and creative ways to express love and appreciation in my partner's preferred language.*

By going beyond the basics, we infuse our connection with vitality, care, and endless joy."

Tread softly upon the sacred ground of togetherness, for it is here that the seeds of spiritual unity germinate, nurtured by the tender waters of mutual dedication. Within the embrace of matrimonial harmony, we discover that true intimacy is far more than the convergence of two bodies; it is, indeed, the alchemy of souls entwined in a dance as ancient as time itself.

As we journey forth hand in hand, hearts beating as one, let us declare with fervent assurance an affirmation of spiritual unity that resonates with the truths we hold dear. With every breath, let our love be a beacon that lights the path of righteousness and grace, guiding us with an unwavering resolve to honor the essence of our sacred bond.

In this silent sanctuary of intimacy, let our whispers become the hymns that honor the divine tapestry of our love. We affirm to speak life into our partnership, to sow words of encouragement that bloom into bouquets of affirmation. Like an artist with a palette of infinite hues, we paint our deeds with kindness and our intentions with the colors of generosity.

With gentle strength, we embrace the wisdom that every moment shared, every tear shed, and every smile exchanged, are threads in a quilt that wraps us in the warmth of each other's spirit. We cherish the silent language of understanding, the glances, and gestures that speak volumes where words are mere echoes in the vast chamber of our union.

As we bask in the glow of spiritual kinship, let us remember that each day offers renewed vows, a chance to reaffirm our commitment to walk through the valleys and ascend the peaks together. Through the serene and the tumultuous, we hold fast to the conviction that the love we share is a lighthouse in the fog, a steadfast promise of safe harbor.

Our unity in intimacy weaves a narrative that transcends the temporal. It is not merely ink on the pages of our history but the living prose that narrates our existence. This unity is our fortress, forged in the craftsmanship of trust, adorned with the tapestry of shared dreams and aspirations.

This bond is our legacy, a testament to the enduring power of love sustained by the mutual reverence of our spirit. We honor it by tending to the garden of our relationship, pruning away the weeds of doubt, and watering the soil with the essence of fidelity and respect.

For in the fabric of our togetherness, each stitch bears witness to a promise woven with the golden threads of eternity. We stand, not as two separate beings, but as one entity bound by an unbreakable vow, a covenant that echoes in the sacred halls of our togetherness.

Let us carry forward this profound affirmation into the days ahead, keeping ablaze the fire of our union, even as the winds of change blow and the seasons turn. Our love, a river rich with the currents of passion and devotion, flows endlessly towards the horizon of shared tomorrows.

And as we gaze upon the dawning of a new chapter in our joint narrative, let us step forward with courage, buoyed by the knowledge that even when we grapple with adversity, we possess the fortitude and wisdom to transform disputes into bridges of understanding. It is with this spirit that we transcend the ordinary, weaving an ever-evolving tapestry of love that stands as a monument to the spiritual essence of intimacy—a love that shapes, defines, and refines us in the crucible of life's experiences, leading us magnificently into the unfolding story of 'The Art of Constructive Conflict.

6

Flourishing in Shared Abundance

Spiritual and Financial Abundance

Bethune Graphics

Prosperity Through Spiritual and Financial Unity

PRINCIPLE: In unity, there is abundance; aligning spiritual and financial growth paves the way for a thriving union.

BLISS PROTOCOL #16: Creating Shared Rituals

- **Scenario:** Lack of meaningful traditions
- **Solution:** Ritual development
- **Implementation:** Regular practices
- **Key Advice:** Create sacred traditions

As dawn's tender light unfurls across the horizon, two souls awaken to the day—a canvas upon which they will paint their shared dreams with strokes of determination and splashes of faith. In the gentle clasp of intertwined fingers, they find the reassurance of their shared journey: a path toward flourishing in abundance.

Here, within the sanctuary of their union, they uncover the profound truth that when spiritual and financial growth move in concert, the music of prosperity is not just a sweet serenade but the hymn of a thriving life together.

This journey is not for the faint of heart. It requires the courage to entwine two distinct histories, cultures, and souls into one harmonious narrative. It holds the promise of a garden where the seeds of financial savvy are sown with reverence alongside spiritual virtues, to yield a harvest abundant in tender joys and worldly gains. The essence of our principle—unity birthing abundance—beckons us to embrace truth as old as time: harmony in heart and home is the bedrock of a prosperous marriage.

This chapter is an inviting porch light on the homely abode of matrimony, casting its glow on the steps that lead toward the realignment of our deeper values with our daily strides toward wealth. It's not just about money in the bank; it's about treasures held in trust, endeavors soaked in prayer, and the shared labor of two souls crafting their legacy in rhythm with their heartbeat.

And so, we introduce the fertile chapters that lie ahead—each a step forward in the dance of unity. We will explore the intricacies of harmonizing your deepest values with financial plans, bridging the vast seas of disparities with bridges sturdy with understanding and trust, and crafting a financial plan that sings the melodies of your most sacred aspirations. Our odyssey will take us through the gardens of health and spiritual fortitude, where the wealth of heart and body blooms as resplendently as any currency.

With each turn of the page, you will find a dedication to the rituals and practices that celebrate your love, the milestones proudly achieved, and the synchronicity of two hearts beating as one in pursuit of abundance. Your marriage, a vessel cast upon the waters of life's uncertainty, shall find the winds favorable and currents kind, buoyed as much by faith as by practical wisdom.

We stand on the threshold of discovery, where every word you are poised to read is a stepping stone laid before you, guiding your passage. In these pages, a promise lies waiting to be —a promise that in the unity of your hearts and the constructive interaction of your aspirations, there lies an untapped wellspring of abundance.

As you step forward into this chapter, let it be with hearts wide open, ready to receive the transformation that beckons, ready to affirm, together, a prosperity as infinite as your love.

It is with brave resolve that we embark upon this journey, for the promise of today is written in the legacy of tomorrow. Let this chapter be the light that leads you home—to each other and to the abundant life that awaits. The stage is set; the orchestra is tuned. Let us now behold the first symphony of prosperity.

Harmonizing Material Ambitions with Spiritual Values

In the pursuit of a life filled with love and prosperity, there exists a delicate alchemy that transforms base metals into gold. This alchemy is the art of blending material ambitions with spiritual values, creating a union that is rich in stature and sanctity. It is in this holy space that couples find the strength to draft a shared story of abundance that honors both their earthly needs and heavenly aspirations.

As we go deeper into the marrow of wealth—beyond the surface allure of paper bills and gleaming coins—we discover a realm where prosperity does more than fill our accounts; it fulfills our souls. It's a place where the currency is love and the dividends are paid in the richness of shared purpose and collective growth.

This union of monetary and moral is not a task solely for titans of industry nor saints in seclusion; it is the everyday work of lovers bent on building an empire of the heart.

Imagine a tapestry woven with the vibrant threads of your partner's dreams, both spiritual and material, and your own. With each intertwining strand, a stronger fabric is created—a cloth that can weather the storms of doubt and the winds of fortune with equal grace. Here, talk of budgets and spreadsheets flows as freely as conversations about aspirations and beliefs.

In these dialogues, there is an understanding that their pursuit of wealth is not a sprint toward a pile of riches, but a mutual marathon toward fulfilling each other's dreams, supported by an unwavering faith.

In this sacred confluence, you navigate through decision-making not as solitary agents, but as co-authors of a grand manifesto of abundance. Each choice, from a simple household purchase to significant investments, is infused with the essence of your shared values. It is in this mindful merging that goals are not merely set but sanctified, giving every earned penny a higher purpose and every financial milestone a deeper joy.

The fruit borne of this union is one of resilience, for couples who can dance in harmony to the rhythms of fiscal responsibility and spiritual integrity are not easily shaken. Instead, their roots are anchored deep in shared soil, rich with understanding and nourished by mutual respect. This wealth of spirit becomes the enduring legacy that outshines even the most dazzling of fortunes.

As our reflections on wealth and worth draw to a serene close, we stand at the cusp of new understanding. It is here that the next step of our journey beckons—bridging not just the spiritual with the material but also the differences that may lie between two hearts, two histories, two paths now merged into one. Let us move forward, knowing that the truest form of abundance blooms in the garden where our financial endeavors walk hand in hand with our cherished beliefs, and every step taken is one step closer to a shared paradise.

Bridging Financial Disparities for Marital Harmony

In the sacred dance of matrimony, where two souls strive in unison to the rhythm of shared aspirations, they often encounter a syncopation of means - a financial disparity that, if unbridled, can taint the sweetest of melodies. This disparity need not be a discord, but rather, it can transform into a harmonious chord that enriches the song of togetherness, bonding partners even closer as they navigate their shared fiscal landscape with compassion and wisdom.

In the quiet of a shared space, where vulnerability is not a weakness but a bridge to deeper intimacy, it is here that couples must summon the courage to unveil the ledgers of their lives, baring to each other not merely the numbers that define their wealth, but the fears, hopes, and dreams that those numbers represent. This is the heart of openness, where transparency becomes the cornerstone of a financial union built not on the sands of secrecy but on the bedrock of mutual trust.

It is incumbent upon each partner to step into the other's financial shoes, to comprehend the journey that has shaped their understanding of wealth. It is through such empathetic exploration that the whispers of judgment give way to the chorus of understanding, and from this understanding blooms a collective vision of financial harmony.

Together, amid the ebb and flow of life's economic tides, one learns to buoy the other, ensuring that every storm encountered is weathered side by side, as equals in both struggle and triumph.

Within these shared confidences, a strategy of love and finance unfurls—one that does not seek to outshine the other in earnings or acumen but instead aspires to uplift both to new heights of abundance. Practical tools of budgeting and investments become instruments played in concert, and the mundane task of reconciling bank statements transforms into a duet of dedication that reinforces the bond of matrimony.

As couples commence this journey of collaborative economics, they begin to realize the potency of their partnership, wielding their combined fiscal energies to cultivate a climate of growth and generosity within their union. It is not solely prosperity that they chase, but wealth that is magnified by its impact on their shared dreams and the love that melds those dreams into reality.

The currency of compassion, coupled with the wealth of wisdom, casts out the shadows of financial secrecy and inhabits every conversation, decision, and dream with a luminous transparency. It is through this light that couples traverse the path toward a balanced relationship, where cooperation replaces competition, and every financial obstacle surmounted is a testament to the strength of their united spirit.

As they move forward, side by side, in this pilgrimage of fiscal and emotional solidarity, they lay the groundwork for a financial plan that breathes life into their most sacred values. With hearts attuned to the cadence of consciousness, they stand ready to delve into the next chapter of their journey—a chapter whereby the tapestry of their monetary decisions becomes a reflection of their most cherished beliefs, embroidered with the gold thread of spiritual resonance, guiding them toward a shared and prosperous future.

Crafting a Financial Plan that Reflects Shared Spiritual Values

The roots of enduring prosperity intertwine the soil of the spirit with the seeds of financial intention. As couples weave their lives together, creating a tapestry that bears the hues of communal dreams and the essence of individual aspirations, the need for a financial plan infused with shared spiritual values becomes the framework upon which their future is built. It is within the delicate balance of give-

and-take that such a plan emerges, not as a list of cold calculations but as a living document that grows and breathes with the rhythm of their joined hearts.

In this sacred endeavor, couples are called to the table of unity, laying before them the blueprint of their collective economic vision. Here, the conversation flows like a gentle stream, carrying the essence of their beliefs and guiding them to the shores of thoughtful decision-making. Questions that arise are not ones of mere profit, but queries that reach for a higher yield—a yield measured in the currency of joy, peace, and love.

Deliberations become a communion, where each investment, be it in stocks, property, or education, is scrutinized not only for its potential to increase wealth but also for its ability to ferry them closer to realizing their shared destiny. In this sanctuary of finance and faith, giving takes on new depth; it becomes an expression of their collective commitment to the world, a testament to the principles that define who they are, both as individuals and as a partnership.

Philanthropy weaves its golden thread through the fabric of their fiscal discourse, illuminating the path toward a legacy that transcends material accumulation. Charitable endeavors become cornerstones in their fortress of prosperity, not only enriching the lives of others but also fortifying their bond. The joy found in giving, the enrichment of the soul, becomes as important as the growth of their net worth.

Mindful spending, likewise, is not an exercise in frugality but a dance of deliberate choice. Each purchase, no matter how seemingly inconsequential, is an opportunity to affirm their values, celebrate their culture, and contribute to their community. It is in this way that the mundane act of buying transforms into a ceremony of intention—one that resonates with the rich beats of their shared being and the silent melodies of their collective journey.

In these moments, when decisions about money echo the commitments of the soul, a profound alchemy occurs. The ledger lines of income and expenses become a canvas on which their life's work is painted; the portfolio of assets, a gallery displaying their deepest priorities. This is wealth redefined—not merely as an accumulation of resources but as the wise stewardship of those resources in alignment with the spiritual symphony they both conduct.

As couples etch their financial plan with the pen of purpose, they lay a new threshold. Beyond it awaits the flourishing of their well-being, not merely in numerical abundance but in a wealth that envelops, transcends, and encompasses. It is thus with thoughtful hearts and hands joined that they step forward, ready to cultivate together the bountiful garden of their physical health and spiritual prosperity—a garden tended with the utmost care to bear fruits that nourish both body and soul.

Lachele recalls the pivotal period of premarital counseling with her then-fiancé, Kofie, which initially started as couple counseling before transitioning into premarital guidance. This extensive counseling, lasting a year, was crucial for them, especially as it related to financial transparency and vulnerability.

From the onset, Kofie was an open book, willing to share all aspects of his financial life. In contrast, Lachele was more reserved. Despite her love and trust in Kofie, she was initially unwilling to discuss her personal finances, not even with the counselors. "I was not discussing finances, crafting a financial plan, or telling some counselors my personal business about my finances," Lachele admits. This reticence extended to Kofie, to whom she did not disclose her financial details for a year into their marriage.

This lack of financial transparency initially created challenges when they married. While Kofie remained open and vulnerable, Lachele kept to herself, particularly about money matters. "I was talking, but not about finances," she explains. Despite these challenges, Kofie demonstrated great patience and understanding, allowing Lachele the time she needed to open up. It was not until two years into their marriage that she felt comfortable enough to begin merging their finances.

During this period, they faced additional challenges, such as differing views on tithing, which was important to Lachele but not practiced by Kofie initially. However, they managed these differences with grace and mutual respect, discussing their budget monthly even though they hadn't fully merged their finances.

Reflecting on their journey, Lachele appreciates Kofie's unwavering commitment and the respect they cultivated for each other's perspectives on money and stewardship. "Now, I can say that we do merge our money, and it's because of the respect we have for each other and the respect we have about money and stewardship that has made it very amicable between the two of us," she concludes, sharing a laugh about their early budgeting efforts.

This story underscores the importance of time, patience, and respect in aligning financial goals and practices within a marriage, aligning them with shared spiritual values.

Cultivating Abundance in Health and Well-being

In the verdant grove of matrimonial unity, where the limbs of love intertwine with the roots of responsibility, there blooms the fragrant flower of holistic abundance. Health and well-being are the blossoms that signal a marriage flourishing in its entirety—not merely in wealth of pocket but in riches of person and spirit. It is a garden that thrives on the nourishment of shared values, the sunlight of mutual respect, and the water of unwavering support—each element as crucial as the next, culminating in the vitality of a bond unshakeable by life's tempests.

The journey toward cultivating this abundance requires that couples move beyond the ledger of assets to account for the wellness of their being. Financial prosperity, in all its splendor, is but a hollow victory without the health to savor its fruits. Therefore, as two hearts navigate the winding roads of fiscal responsibility, they must also tend to the sacred temple of the body, caring for it with the same diligence and devotion that they apply to their shared coffers.

Together, hand in hand, they are called to explore the rich landscape of nutritional wisdom, to partake in the wholesome bounty that sustains and energizes. Mindful eating becomes a shared ritual, an intentional practice that honors the body as a cherished vessel through which all of life's adventures are experienced. In these daily moments of choosing sustenance, they reaffirm their commitment to a life abundant, engaging in a symphony of flavors that dance upon the tongue and nourish the soul.

Exercise, too, takes its rightful place in the symphony of their union, not as a chore but as a celebration of movement and capability. The shared joy found in a walk through nature's cathedral, the tandem rhythm of hearts beating in unison on a bike ride, or the communal solace found in a restorative yoga session, are the tender threads that knit together a robust tapestry of physical well-being. By celebrating each other's strength, encouraging perseverance, and sympathizing with moments of weariness, they create a bond that is both resilient and supple.

Yet, let not the care for the body overshadow the serenity of the mind. Together, they embark on the path of mindful practices—meditation, introspection, and constructive dialogue—that shape the contours of their inner peace. The quietude cultivated in these shared spaces of reflection becomes a sanctuary from the clamor of the world, a place where their spirits can commune, unburdened by the cacophony of external demands.

Financial acumen and spiritual growth, health, and happiness, all intertwine to form the quilt of their collective abundance. No thread can stand alone—each is needed to support and enhance the other, creating a warmth that envelopes and protects them from life's chill. Thus, the couple learns that to be truly abundant is to thrive as a confluence of wealth in all its manifestations—financial, physical, emotional, and spiritual.

And so, just as the earth rotates in a graceful, poised pirouette around the sun, they too circle around each other, in the dance of life together. Stirred by the rhythm of shared prosperity, their next steps take them into the realm of celebration, a space where each milestone, each moment of growth, is acknowledged and exalted. Here, they establish the rituals that keep the home fires of abundance burning bright, warming themselves in the glow of all they have, all they are, and all they are yet to become.

Celebrating Prosperity: Rituals and Practices

Connected with the triumphs of diligent care for body and soul, the sanctified union now embarks on a jubilant path of rejoicing in the fruits of shared prosperity. Here, the heart swells with gratitude, and every victory, be it humble or grand, becomes a cause for celebration—the kind of celebration that weaves even closer the spiritual tapestry of a couple's life together.

In this resplendent phase of their journey, couples enshrine their moments of abundance through rituals and practices that serve not only as testament to their love but also as a reaffirmation of their spiritual and financial union. These rituals are the hearthstone of their home, a sacred space heating the air with memories and forging an indelible, communal legacy.

Gratitude practices emerge as the cornerstone of this ritualistic homage to abundance. Reflection upon the day's blessings, voiced in the serenity of dusk or the quietude of dawn, nurtures a profound appreciation for the shared journey. Small, whispered, or written, are like seeds planted in fertile soil—growing into a lush orchard of contentment and peace.

Couples may also engage in the tradition of abundance affirmations, a vocal celebration of their faith in endless prosperity. With words spoken in tandem, echoing through the chambers of their joined hearts, they lay claim to a future as bountiful as it is bright. These affirmations function as guiding stars, illuminating the path toward continued growth and shared ambition, drawing them ever onward in their quest for wholeness.

And what is prosperity without the warmth of shared joy in milestones achieved? Celebrate each breakthrough in financial wisdom, and each attainment of health goals with festivity and flair. These moments, marked by shared laughter and jubilant embraces, etch memories into the timeline of their union, memories that will sparkle like jewels when recounted in the golden years of reflection.

Let them establish annual observances to honor significant achievements, be it the freedom from a debt long-held or a well-crafted investment maturing. These observances are not merely anniversaries of material success but festivals of the tenacity, unity, and dedication that paved the way to each accomplishment. In recognizing these triumphs together, the couple threads another stitch through the fabric of their shared life narrative, binding them in the richness of prosperity experienced and savored as one.

Such shared rituals and practices are the rhythms by which a couple's life together measures time—each beat a testament to the loving labor they've poured into cultivating a life abundant in meaning and rich in purpose. Engaging in these activities is not just about forming a habit but a reaffirmation of their commitment to growing together, both fiscally and spiritually.

In the serene afterglow of celebration, they stand side by side, drawing a deep breath before the next crescendo of their symphony—the affirmation of prosperous unity. It is within this sacred space that the couple weaves the final threads of this chapter, a passage that leads them to both look inward and reach outward, embracing all the vibrancy and vitality that their shared abundance has brought them. With this, their hearts are full, and they know that the tapestry of their life together, illustrious and endearing, stretches forth with promise and expectation, eager for the continuation of their love's enduring song.

Affirmation of Prosperous Unity

Just as two harmonious notes blend to create a chord more beautiful than the sum of its parts, so too does the fusion of spiritual depth and financial insight forge a union resplendent with promise. In this sacred coda of our journey, we affirm the melody of prosperous unity, a chord struck deeply in the hearts and souls of those entwined in matrimonial harmony.

Let it be spoken, let it be felt: we stand at the precipice of an ever-expanding horizon, hands clasped and eyes alight with the shared vision of a future woven from threads of unyielding trust, and unshakeable faith. With every breath, with every beat of our collective heart, we affirm our alliance to the covenant of love and the prosperity it nurtures within and around us.

As we draw upon the reservoir of rituals and practices that celebrate our togetherness, let us now seal those joys with a pronouncement of our commitment to the flourishing of shared abundance. We recognize that true wealth is found not in the clamor of coins but in the whispers of contentment, in the power of shared aspirations, and in the tenderness of unwavering support that nourishes the very essence of our bonded spirits.

We acknowledge that this path is neither short nor devoid of challenge. Yet, as guardians of each other's dreams, we pledge to walk it with integrity and grace, anchoring ourselves in the belief that together, adversity will be but a shadow against the luminosity of our united purpose. May our path be lit with the lanterns of wisdom gleaned from each trial and the warmth of victories savored in the quiet sanctum of our communion.

As the fabric is strengthened by the interweaving of every thread, so is the fabric of our marriage enhanced through the shared ideology of prosperity that transcends the mundane. We, as a couple, uphold a legacy—a heritage embroidered with resilience, adorned with cultural significance, and steeped in an ancestral spirituality that carries us forward on wings of progress.

In this shared breath of existence, we craft an affirmation so potent it becomes the very air around us.

"We affirm our commitment to each other and to our collective well-being; spiritually, emotionally, physically, and financially. We stand together in the light of faith, and the unequivocal belief that our unity is our greatest asset. We pledge to cultivate this bond, to treasure it, and to allow it to guide us towards mutual prosperity and a life resplendent with joy."

This affirmation is our compass; it directs us toward the fulfillment of our deepest desires and aspirations. It is a pledge to continual evolution, an ode to the rhythm of life that beckons us to the dance of purposeful collaboration—a collaboration that not only our own lives but casts ripples of positivity throughout our community.

As we breathe life into this affirmation, we understand that our journey does not pause; it simply evolves, flowing seamlessly toward the next chapter of our shared story—a chapter that beckons us to delve even deeper into the essence of matrimonial unity and well-being. With the affirmation of prosperous unity beating like a drum in our souls, we step into the dawning light of a new day, where the embrace of physical and spiritual growth awaits us.

Here, in the tender space between heartbeats, we find the grace to nurture every dimension of our united existence, and we carry with us the knowing that our love, ever so cherished, is the key to unlocking the boundless harmonies of health in marriage.

7

Embracing Unified Purpose

Unified in Purpose

MK Photography

Synergizing Dreams into a Shared Journey

PRINCIPLE: "Two souls, one journey; embracing a unified purpose is the essence of true partnership."

BLISS PROTOCOL #1: Rediscovering Your Why:

- **Scenario:** Loss of connection to original purpose
- **Solution:** Reconnection with foundational values
- **Implementation:** Story sharing, value exploration
- **Key Advice:** Return to your love story's origins

Upon the sacred canvas of marriage, two souls are called to paint a masterpiece, where the colors of individual dreams blend seamlessly to create a shared vision, as vibrant and enduring as the very journey of life itself. It is within this harmonious merger that the true essence of partnership takes flight, soaring on the wings of unified purpose, and declaring to the world that together, we are stronger, wiser, and more luminous than we could ever be apart.

As we delve into the heart of this chapter, let us be reminded that each stroke of the brush, each hue selected, is an intentional choice that shapes our shared destiny. For in the art of marriage, it is not only love that binds us; it is the commitment to a common goal, a collective ambition that sings the melody of alignment, resonance, and a promise to journey through every season side by side.

The seeds of a dream, when sown in the fertile soil of togetherness, bloom into a bountiful harvest of achievement and jubilation. This is our guiding axiom; the principle that "Two souls, one journey; embracing a unified purpose is the essence of true partnership." It is this conviction that shall illuminate the path for us as we navigate through the tapestry of chapters outlined before us.

We begin with the Power of Shared Dreams. Here, you'll uncover the cornerstone of marital strength—how to recognize, cherish, and elevate the aspirations that each partner brings to the table. In the sacred dance of matrimony, each step is a declaration of our shared intent and a vow to lift each other up as we reach for the stars.

Balancing Aspirations: The Art of Inclusion beckons us to the intricacies of love and life, where we shall discover the elegance of weaving individual desires into a fabric that embraces and honors both parties. It is a canvas painted with strokes of compromise, understanding, and the art of listening to our beloved's voice as attentively as we do our own.

In Harmonizing Voices: Communication and Support, the symphony of matrimony finds its rhythm. This is where words unsaid hold as much power as those spoken aloud, where the soul's deepest yearnings find their echo in our partner's embrace, and where encouragement becomes our guiding light through the ebb and flow of life's endless river.

Aligning Paths: Navigating Differences Together navigates the treacherous yet transcendent terrain where divergent dreams converge upon a single road. It is the invitation to join hands, respect disparities, and journey onward with an unwavering commitment to our shared spiritual growth.

The penultimate movement in our symphony, Crafting the Vision: Building a Future Together, teaches us the architect's craft, as we draft the blueprints of our shared dreams. This chapter summons us to the drafting table to draw, with careful deliberations and heartfelt passion, the contours of a future that belongs to both.

And we shall pave the final stretch of our journey with Living the Dream: Implementing the Shared Vision. It speaks of moving beyond dreaming, beyond the planning into the sacred realm where action breathes life into our collective aspirations. Here, the vibrant tapestry we've woven comes alive, animated by our unwavering determination, and adorned with the milestones of our success.

So, let us set forth with the promise that this chapter holds—to weave our dreams into a shared journey, to honor the unique melodies of our individual spirits while composing a symphony of togetherness. For in the harmonious blend of our souls' desires, in the sweet whispers of shared dreams, lies the promise of a lifetime filled with love, understanding, and a purpose that transcends the very essence of time.

Together, we shall embark on this journey, hearts aligned and spirits united, as we turn the pages of our lives and discover the beauty of Embracing Unified Purpose.

Balancing Aspirations: The Art of Inclusion

In this powerful chapter, we turn to the sacred task of weaving the strands of our separate dreams into the quilt of our united destiny. The art of inclusion is not just a practice but a pledge; a vow that within our bond, every ambition, and every hope one holds will find fertile ground to grow, under the sheltering sky of our shared love and purpose.

Imagine, if you will, standing at the juncture of two roads, each representing the aspirations you and your partner harbor within your hearts. Now see yourself, not at a crossroads of decision, but at the merging of these paths into one that leads to a horizon bright with potential. This vision can only materialize when we, with concerted effort and boundless love, master the delicate art of embracing both sets of aspirations, weaving them into a tapestry that bears the mark of both your spirits.

To include is to acknowledge. To acknowledge is to respect. And to respect is to amplify the beauty of your union, enabling each dream to resonate with the strength of your combined passions. The collective journey of matrimony should not be a solitary climb up a steep mountainside, but a journey through verdant valleys and over majestic peaks, hand in hand, with the embers of individual dreams casting a shared warmth.

Within these pages, discover the stories that echo your own—the tales of those who have danced the intricate steps of inclusion and emerged with a partnership robust in its diversity. Learn how to express your desires without drowning out the melodies of your partner's voice. Cultivate a dialogue that is a duet, harmonizing the distinct tunes of your individual dreams into a chorus that uplifts and carries both of you toward your shared aspirations.

But inclusion goes beyond mere acknowledgment—it requires action. To truly include is to advocate for each other's dreams with the same fervor as our own. It is to become the custodian of your partner's aspirations and to feel a sense of joy in each stride they take towards their goals, knowing that their triumphs are your shared celebrations.

Here, you'll also find the practical wisdom to navigate the moments when dreams diverge, and the waters seem tumultuous. Together, we'll explore strategies to steer your collective vessel through both calm and storm, ensuring that the sails of your individual aspirations always catch the winds of encouragement and understanding.

As you stand shoulder to shoulder, gaze upon the ebb and flow of time and life, remember that it is your shared aspirations that anchor you in the currents. Embracing each other's dreams is the song of resilience—it is the melody that will resonate through your lives, imbuing them with meaning, direction, and the profound understanding that your love is a journey not of two paths but one.

It is in the embrace of this truth we find our greatest strength. So let us step forward, taking in hand the brush and palette, ready to paint the next stroke on our canvas of shared existence. As we journey onward, let us prepare to lend an ear to the symphony of our voices, in dialogue, support, and unwavering affirmation of one another's intrinsic value.

We move forward, not into a negotiation of dreams, but into the grace of mutual encouragement, where neither voice is lost, but both are amplified in the echo chamber of our hearts' deepest chambers. And in this resonant space, we find not only the key to balancing aspirations but to fulfilling them in the embrace of a shared journey that honors every step of our individual and collective growth.

Harmonizing Voices: Communication and Support

In the tapestry of marriage, each thread tells a story, each strand a shared note in the melody of matrimony. As we nurture the art of inclusion, the natural progression leads us to the sanctum of effective communication—the cadence that ensures our voices blend harmoniously, rather than clashing in dissonance. Within the symphony of our partnership, each voice must be heard, each story must resonate with a tender timbre of understanding.

Communication, when rooted in love and respect, becomes the bridge that connects the islands of our individuality. It grants us passage to the inner sanctum of our partner's hopes and fears. In this sacred act, we find strength not in speaking, but in listening—truly listening—with a heart open to the silent songs of our beloved's soul. We listen not to reply, but to comprehend; to echo back with the fullness of empathy that says, "I hear you, I understand you, and your dreams matter deeply to me."

Support is the lifeblood that flows through the veins of this communion. It is the quiet strength that whispers encouragement in moments of doubt and the steady hand that upholds our partner's ambition when the weight seems too much to bear alone. When we support one another, we become the lighthouse guiding each other back to our shared shores, especially when the mist of uncertainty seeks to obscure our way.

Pause for a moment and imagine the depth of trust that blooms from the soil of genuine communication and unconditional support. It is here, in this garden of trust, where dreams are shared without fear, where aspirations become a common quest, and where every victory is a stone in the foundation of our collective progress.

How then do we cultivate this garden? By watering our conversations with kindness, by pruning the thorns of misunderstanding with patience, and by shining the sunlight of clarity onto our shared path. As we journey forward, let us remember the importance of affirmation—for each "I believe in you" is like a balm that heals past wounds and a beacon that shines on future achievements.

The art and science of communication are not reserved for the grand declarations of love and progress; they are found in the quiet moments, the simple acts of presence and acknowledgment that say, "You are seen, you are valued, and you are not alone in this journey." It is the attentive glance, the gentle squeeze of the hand, and the shared laughter that dances between two hearts in unison.

As we delve deeper into the realms of connection, let us also embrace the diversity of our expressions. For what is love, if not the appreciation of each unique brushstroke that paints the masterpiece of our united yet distinct existence?

Embrace the dialogue that emboldens, understands, and transforms. Share the dreams that stir the soul and watch as, together, you ascend the staircase of your aspirations, each step a testament to your mutual dedication and the joyous affirmation of your commitment.

With hearts synchronized to the rhythm of each other's yearning, let us journey forth, bearing the mantle of mutual reverence. It is through the binding threads of conversation, comfort, and unwavering encouragement that we construct the narrative of our lives—a narrative that leads us, hand in hand, into the open embrace of navigating our differences together, where our pathways converge into harmonious understanding.

Aligning Paths: Navigating Differences Together

As we journey down the road of lifelong commitment, clasping the hand of our beloved, we recognize that our footprints are unique, each step an expression of our individual identity. Yet, the beauty of this journey lies not in walking a singular path, but in aligning our paths—two souls on a pilgrimage towards a horizon ripe with shared purpose and collective dreams.

There exists a sweetness in the discovery that, while our paths may diverge, they can be navigated together through the verdant landscapes of compromise and mutual respect. It is akin to a dance, where each step, each pirouette, is a testament to our shared rhythm, a rhythm that can accommodate the beats of two different drums harmonizing into a singular symphony.

This alignment requires attentiveness to the other's movements, a readiness to sway when they sway, to advance when they move forward, and to pause with tender patience when they need to catch their breath. It demands that we learn the choreography of their heart's deepest longings and allow space for their dreams to twirl freely alongside our own.

What do we do when our dreams seem like stars in different galaxies, far-flung across the celestial canvas of our desires? We take comfort in the knowledge that the night sky is vast, and there is ample room for our stars to shine brightly without dimming the radiance of the other. We chart a course guided by the constellations of our mutual aspirations, discovering that it is possible for our dreams to coexist, to be in dialogue with each other, and to even illuminate the path forward for both.

Navigating differences is akin to tending a garden of diverse flora. It is recognizing that a rose's beauty does not threaten the sunflower's stature. Similarly, the robustness of our personal goals does not diminish our partner's ambitions. Instead, we work together to till the soil, to water each seed with the nourishment of encouragement, and to cultivate an environment where both can flourish, side by side, in an eclectic yet harmonious garden.

To navigate our differences is to embrace the ebb and flow of our journey, understanding that there will be times of serene waters and times when the rapids challenge our resolve. It is in these moments that our bond is evaluated, but also strengthened, as we come to realize that love is not simply a feeling, but an act of will—a conscious decision to row the vessel of our union with synchronized determination.

As we lift our gaze to the shared summits of our aspirations, let us also cherish the valleys—the tender, vulnerable spaces where we learn more about ourselves and each other. For it is within these moments of introspection that we uncover the resilience to ascend any peak, comforted by the warmth of our intertwined hands and the heartbeat of our collective courage.

We may find that our paths intersect at unexpected junctures, and it is here, amid the crossroads of our individual dreams, that we discover opportunities for growth and depth that we had not dared to imagine alone. In this union, we are offered the rare chance to transform the tapestry of our shared existence into a kaleidoscopic tableau of love, purpose, and mutual triumph.

So, let us tread gently yet confidently into this dance of alignment, where differences are not just tolerated but celebrated as the vibrant hues that add depth to the masterpiece we create together. With each step, with each shared dream, we weave a bond that is both resilient and supple, ready to bend with the winds of change without breaking.

And hand in hand, as we continue this journey, let us move with grace toward the canvas of our future, where we will paint a vision so vast and beautiful, it can only be realized with the brushstrokes of two hearts working in tandem. This vision—our vision—awaits us just over the horizon, beckoning us to approach with bold strokes of bravery and tender touches of love.

Crafting the Vision: Building a Future Together

In the sacred bonds of matrimony, our hearts are the compasses that guide us toward crafting a vision rich with possibilities, a future meticulously painted with broad strokes of unity and delicate touches of individuality. This shared vision—a mosaic of dreams—requires us to lay each piece with intention, understanding that every hue and texture represents a part of our shared story.

Crafting this vision is like gathering the warmth of sunshine in our hands, feeling its potential to grow the seeds we've planted in the fertile soil of our commitment. As we sit across from each other, our knees touching and our souls bared, we hold the sacred space to dream aloud, to sketch the outlines of a future that honors both the 'I' and the 'we' in our partnership.

Begin where the heart sings loudest, where passion and purpose intertwine like the intertwining roots of an ancient tree. Here we ask, "What are your heart's deepest desires?" and listen with an ear tuned to the whispers of our partner's spirit. It is a conversation held not only with words but with the language of understanding, a vernacular shaped by shared glances and knowing smiles.

The vision we build should be resilient, a fortress against the storms of life, yet flexible enough to sway with the winds of change. It should be expansive, like the open sky, providing room for each of our dreams to soar on the wings of possibility. We etch our aspirations into the walls of this fortress with the knowledge that, together, we are architects of our destiny.

From each shared dream a blueprint emerges, spacious and brimming with potential. We plot the milestones, not merely as destinations but as signposts of progress along the winding road of life's grand journey. These milestones are the echoes of our love, reverberating through time, reminding us of the places our combined energy has carried us.

As we deliberate over this blueprint, consider the principles that fortify the foundation—trust, understanding, compromise, and faith. These are the pillars upon which our vision rests. These principles are the sacred vows we renew each day, not merely through words spoken at the altar of commitment but through actions woven into the tapestry of daily life.

Crafting a vision together also means recognizing when to lead and when to follow, when to assert, and when to yield. It's in the give and take, the rhythmic dance of balance, that we find harmony. It's in the small, shared victories and the quiet concessions, where love manifests its truest form, humble and

In the process of creating a shared future, there may be times when the picture seems incomplete or the colors blur. Do not despair, for this is simply an invitation to reach deeper into our reservoir of love, to fetch the water that will clarify our vision. It is during these moments that we are reminded of the eternal nature of love, an art forever in progress, each stroke of challenge adding depth to the beauty we create together.

And so, let us take each other's hands, our fingers laced with the threads of yesterday's hopes and tomorrow's promises, and step bravely into the canvas of our making. Let us paint boldly, with broad strokes of trust and fine lines of dedication, knowing that each day brings us closer to the reality of our collective dreams.

As we conclude this chapter of shared vision, let it be known that the journey forward is not a solitary quest, but one enriched by the warmth of shared aspirations. It is a pathway illuminated by the golden light of unity, leading us towards not only the fulfillment of our dreams but also the realization of a deeper connection, mutual support that paves the way toward actualizing our aspirations and breathing life into the vision we've so lovingly crafted together.

Our Story

In discussing the importance of building a future together, we've come to understand the critical role of crafting a shared vision. The very reason two people come together in marriage is to create a unified path forward.

Creating a shared vision for your future involves laying out practical steps to articulate and plan your common goals and dreams. Too often in marriages, spouses move in different directions, like ships passing in the night. However, if you can come together and discuss your individual passions, you should be able to unite in a spirit of teamwork, sharing aspirations and helping each other achieve goals that build a future together.

It's easy when you're single to focus solely on your own desires, as you have no one else to consider. However, marriage requires considering your partner in all decisions. Building a future together involves sitting down, writing out a plan, and carefully considering the costs and direction of your shared journey.

We find guidance in Habakkuk 2:2-3, which says, "And the Lord answered me: 'Write the vision; make it plain on tablets, so he may run who reads it. For still the vision awaits its appointed time; it hastens to the end—it will not lie. If it seems slow, wait for it; it will surely come; it will not delay.'"

This scripture reinforces the importance of not just one person working on the marriage, but both partners being involved. By writing down the vision and making it clear, both can align with and pursue it. If both partners agree on the unity they want to share, then counting the cost becomes essential in unifying what each person needs to contribute to the marriage.

In essence, building a future together is about clear communication, shared goal-setting, and mutual commitment to the vision you create as a couple. It's a process that requires ongoing dialogue, compromise, and a willingness to work together toward common dreams and aspirations.

Living the Dream: Implementing the Shared Vision

Embodying the dream that was once whispered in the stillness of two interlocked hearts requires action that beats to the drum of our deepest convictions. It is in Living the Dream, in the steadfast pursuit of our shared vision, that the true spirit of our unity is given flight—lifting from the realm of imagination and soaring into the tapestry of reality.

The journey ahead, set against the backdrop of a shared skyline, is lined with the stones of intention and action, each one a deliberate step towards manifesting our collective ambitions. It is a pathway not just conceived in the quiet of earnest discussions but also traveled through everyday acts of love and dedication. A prayer whispered in unison, a financial plan meticulously crafted at the kitchen table, a career aspiration supported by unwavering encouragement—these are the building blocks of our living vision.

As we embark on this road, hand in hand, we recognize that our shared dream is a living entity—it breathes with our compromises, grows with our understanding, and thrives on our mutual support. The trials we encounter are but the resistance needed to strengthen the wings of our shared purpose, each challenge is an opportunity to refine and reaffirm our journey toward fulfillment.

The implementation of our shared vision also nestles in the nurturing of our individual strengths. The unique melodies of our souls, when played together, create a symphony of formidable beauty. It is essential, then, to champion each other's talents, and to create space for solo performances that contribute to the grand opus of our collective narrative.

We celebrate each milestone, for it represents a chorus of victories—the harmonizing of our efforts culminating in joyous achievement. These milestones, whether they be the purchase of a home that echoes with future laughter, the attainment of educational pursuits that elevate our understanding, or the simple, profound act of nurturing our spiritual growth—each is savored as a testament to the strength of our union and the grace of divine favor.

Yet, we must also be nimble in our steps, ready to pivot and sway with the changing rhythms of our existence. Adaptability becomes our ally, the recognition that our vision may take on new shapes and forms as we evolve individually and together. The constancy of change does not deter us; instead, it is an affirmation of our commitment to dance to the ever-changing beat of life's grand ballad.

In this dance, we find joy in the shared moments that thread our days together, in the laughter that echoes through the corridors of our home, and in the quiet understanding that passes between us without utterance. Our love story, an ever-unfolding narrative, gathers strength not just from the chapters of triumph but also from the passages that detail our resilience.

As we journey through this implementation of our vision, let us hold tight to the belief that our collective dreams are taking root in the fertile ground of effort and faith. For it is in the tender cultivation of this shared plot of aspirations that the fruits of our labor will one day bloom in abundance, a vibrant testament to the constructive collaboration of our dreams.

And with gratitude, we anticipate the moment when our hands—etched with the years of partnership and perseverance—will turn the page to the next chapter of our quest. It is with hope-filled eyes and hearts brimming with courage that we inch closer to the dawn of realization, where our shared dedication finds its truest expression in the vibrant reality we shape together.

Affirmation of Shared Commitment

Embracing Unified Purpose: Synergizing Dreams into a Shared Journey

Affirmation: *As we navigate the shared journey of marriage, it is vital to reaffirm our commitment not only to each other but also to our collective spiritual mission. This commitment forms the bedrock upon which we build a future marked by mutual love, respect, and divine purpose.*

Affirmation Based on Ecclesiastes 4:9

"Two are better than one, for they have a good return for their labor. Together, we stand stronger, our endeavors amplified by our unity. In this sacred partnership, we commit to support, uplift, and strengthen one another, always striving towards our shared goals under God's gracious guidance."

This affirmation is a powerful declaration of unity. It celebrates the beauty of growing together and underscores the importance of a shared vision. By embracing this affirmation, couples can reinforce their dedication to a path that honors their love and their faith, ensuring that every step taken is one of mutual respect and collective purpose.

"We reconnect with our love story, values, and dreams, rediscovering the 'why' that brought us together. By reigniting our shared sense of purpose, we deepen our appreciation for one another and strengthen our bond."

Standing at the threshold of a collective future, we are reminded that the act of marriage is akin to the joining of two rivers—separate in their origin, yet destined to create an ocean of shared experiences, aspirations, and triumphs. It is within this confluence that the essence of our unity is both tested and affirmed. We hear the echoes of our vows and the silent promises we make each other in the night's hush, we find the strength to affirm our shared commitment to the vision we have so tenderly crafted.

With hearts intertwined, we speak aloud the time-honored words, an echo of Ecclesiastes 4:9, "Two are better than one, for they have a good return for their labor." These words, steeped in wisdom and spoken with the fullness of belief, serve as a compass pointing us toward the true north of our union. Together, with each step in our communal journey, we find a bounty that is greater than the sum of our individual efforts—our labor of love yielding a harvest of joy and purpose that nourishes not only our spirits but the spirits of generations to come.

This affirmation is our guiding star, a lighthouse standing unwavering in the shifting sands of life's shoreline. It reminds us of the beautiful tapestry we are weaving—with threads of laughter, beams of shared wisdom, and knots of challenges overcome. As we stand hand in hand, our collective endeavors become amplified by the strength found in our togetherness, each achievement a stone laid in the foundation of our shared future.

In the daily rhythms of our lives, we renew our commitment to support, uplift, and strengthen one another. We recognize that this covenant is sustained not just by the grand gestures but more so by the quiet acts of kindness—the morning cup of coffee served with tenderness, the listening ear offered after a day of toil, the gentle touch that says "I am here, with you, for you."

And yet, beyond the sanctuary of our home and the intimacy of our shared dreams, we also pledge to cultivate a legacy that extends outward, touching the hearts of our community. We endeavor to be a harbor of hope and a beacon of resilience for those who sail the often tumultuous seas of life. Our love story thus becomes more than a personal narrative; it is a parable of faith, an example of the power of a bond grounded in shared purpose and spiritual conviction.

As we honor this shared commitment, we understand that our path forward is both a journey and a destination. It is an invitation to explore the depths of our being, to forge a partnership that is both a fortress and a garden—fortified by the values we hold dear and blooming with the flowers of our combined growth and aspirations.

And so, we move forward with the assurance that, under God's gracious guidance, our steps are aligned with a purpose greater than ourselves. Our partnership, a vessel filled with the waters of faith and love, sails toward horizons bright with the promise of days yet to unfold. Every sunrise beckons us to new adventures, new challenges, and new joys—a vibrant expression of our unified presence in the world.

With this passage, we stand on the cusp of newfound horizons, ready to step into the embrace of a new chapter. It is with hope and anticipation that we carry the torch of our shared dreams, allowing the flame of our commitment to illuminate the way. Together, we journey on, hearts ablaze with the love that binds us, spirits soaring with the dreams we have dared to dream—united and unyielding in the pursuit of our joint destiny.

8

Nurturing Physical and Spiritual Well-being

Physical and Spiritual health

MK Photography

Harnessing the Harmony of Health in Marriage

PRINCIPLE "Well-being is a harmonious blend of physical health and spiritual depth; nurturing both leads to a flourishing life together."

BLISS PROTOCOL #15: Self-Love and Self-Care:

- **Scenario:** Individual neglect affecting relationship
- **Solution:** Personal wellness practices
- **Implementation:** Individual growth plans
- **Key Advice:** Care for self to care for marriage

In the sacred dance of matrimony, where two hearts beat in rhythmic synchrony, lies the profound potential of holistic well-being—a togetherness that doesn't just survive the squalls but thrives, blossoming like a rose among life's thorns. This chapter is a journey, an embrace of that combined strength, an ode to the principle that "Well-being is a harmonious blend of physical health and spiritual depth; nurturing both leads to a flourishing life together."

It is within the crucible of this understanding that we discover not just the vitality of the body, but the vibrancy of the soul, crafting a symphony of well-being that resonates through the core of our unions.

As we traverse these pages, you and your beloved are invited to stand shoulder to shoulder, hand in hand, committing to a shared path of physical vitality and spiritual enlivenment. It is a promise, a composite of actions and intentions, which weaves a resilient tapestry capable of bearing the weight of the world, yet delicate enough to be buoyed by the whisper of a prayer.

Within this chapter lies the promise of a renewed intimacy, not just of your bodies entwined but of your spirits intertwined, as you embark on joint journeys to physical wellness. We'll explore the deep well from which you both can drink—a wellspring of nourishment for the body and soul.

From the mindfulness that permeates the mundane—the sacred pauses during the chaos—to the spiritual dimensions of health that color your everyday existence, this is a voyage towards a shared horizon.

Our guided exploration will venture through the intertwined paths of sustenance and spirituality, savoring the sustenance that is as nurturing to the body as it is fulfilling to the spirit. In this crucible, the ordinary moments are transmuted into extraordinary memories, where a shared glance over a simple meal becomes a silent conversation of the soul, and where the shared struggles and triumphs forge an unbreakable bond.

As we map this journey, our vision encompasses not just the immediate, tangible aspects of health but extends its gaze to the future, where the seeds of financial well-being you plant today blossom into a garden of abundance and security. It is in this garden that the fruits of your labor will flourish, shared in joy, and savored in the quiet moments of reflection.

With every step forward on this path, with every lesson shared and learned, you will find yourselves weaving an affirmation of holistic harmony—an affirmation that resonates with every fiber of your beings, galvanizing your commitment to each other and to the sanctity of your marital bliss.

Embark on this chapter, dear hearts, with the knowledge that every word is a stepping stone towards the holistic well-being that awaits you. Let it be a compass that guides you away from the fragmented wellness of yore and towards the seamless state of health and spiritual unity that is your birthright.

It is the beacon that illuminates the path, the promise of a life where every breath is a testament to the love you share, and every heartbeat is an affirmation of your collective strength. Let us begin.

Joint Journeys to Physical Wellness: Fortifying Bonds Through Shared Strides

In the mosaic of marriage, every shared stride in physical wellness is a brushstroke on the canvas of your union, a testament to the intention and dedication that underpins your collective journey. The march toward well-being is one that beckons you both to step in tandem, synchronizing your beats to the metronome of health and spiritual solidarity.

Embarking on this path together, the brisk morning jogs become sacred rituals, where each breath you take is a silent vow, a commitment to the longevity of your love and legacy. Yoga mats unfurl like scrolls of unspoken promises, and with each stretch, each pose held in the quietude of dawn or the calm of dusk, your bodies speak an ancient language of unity and peace.

It is not simply the act of moving that fortifies your bond but the infusion of intention that elevates these joint journeys to acts of spiritual communion. Each shared exertion and synchronized heartbeat is a pilgrimage, a soulful venture towards a shrine of well-being that you both revere.

Within these shared practices, be they meditative walks or synchronized breaths, resides the potential to not only shape your body but also to etch the contours of your inner temples.

Here, in the communion of physical effort and spiritual introspection, you will discover the alchemy of joint wellness—where sweat becomes the anointing oil that sanctifies your efforts, and movement becomes the prayer that propels you forward. In the whisper of rubber on asphalt or the silent symphony of a hike through nature's cathedral, there is a shared language of love and aspiration.

It is in these shared jaunts towards wellness that you will find yourselves laying the foundations of health upon which your marriage stands strong. It is a fortress, impervious to the storms of life, built upon the sweat equity of a partnership that values physical prowess as much as the endurance of the heart.

As we journey through this passage, let each step be a moment of rediscovery, an opportunity to gain experience undulating rhythms of your partner; to cherish the contours of their strengths, and extend a hand during a throbbing of a challenging climb. Embrace these shared pursuits as opportunities to forge an indelible connection, one that transcends the flesh and speaks to the essence of your spirits.

As the horizon of this discussion broadens, it gently ushers in an understanding that the sustenance of the body and the fulfillment of the soul are not siloed endeavors but, indeed, are interconnected in the most profound of ways. With each mile walked side by side, you reaffirm a dedication that echoes far beyond the confines of the physical pathways you traverse.

And so, as we ascend from the valleys of our daily routines to the peaks of holistic fulfillment, we remember that the journey itself holds as much beauty as the destination. Let these shared paths of physical wellness be your sacred spaces, where love is both the journey and the destination.

And as we catch our breath, poised at the peak of this shared climb, we position ourselves to explore deeper still, into the intimate connection between the foods we nourish our bodies with and the ethical values that feed our souls, ever weaving the fabric of our lives more tightly together.

Nourishing the Body and Soul: The Symphony of Sustenance and Spirituality

As we move from the verve of our joint physical pursuits into the sanctity of sacred sustenance, we recognize that the nourishment we offer our bodies is indeed an echo of the reverence we bear for our souls. In the hearth of our homes, the kitchen becomes an altar where the act of feeding becomes a celebration of our shared life, an intimate dance between culture, health, and spirituality.

In the delicate art of choosing what graces our tables and our palates, we find an opportunity to manifest our shared ideals and principles. The foods we savor, rich with the flavors passed down through generations, are not merely sustenance but are imbued with the stories of our ancestors, the wisdom of our elders, and the love that has simmered in our families through time.

Together, we explore the paths of dietary harmony, mindful of the nutrients that build our bodies strong and the traditions that keep our spirits anchored. Each shared meal is a mingling of hearts and flavors, creating a tapestry woven from the threads of our intertwined existences.

It is here, in the cultivation of meals that respect both our bodies and our heritage, that health and spirituality align, each bite a testament to our commitment to live vibrantly and to cherish the legacy we carry forward.

We honor the rhythms and cycles of nature in our kitchens, allowing the seasons to dictate the fresh produce that fills our bowls and fuels our bodies. In this act, we demonstrate a quiet reverence for the world that sustains us, understanding that the nourishment we draw from the earth is a gift not to be squandered but celebrated and shared.

There is a profound beauty in the collective act of breaking bread, where hands that once lifted loads and wiped away tears now cradle spoons and pass plates in a ritual of resilience and unity. In this shared space, the sacred and the every day are interwoven, as stories spill as freely as drinks and laughter rises like steam from a pot on the stove.

The crafting of a meal becomes a joint endeavor steeped in love and intention. It is a thoughtful process where dietary choices become acts of affection, the careful selection of ingredients a tender whisper that speaks, "I care for you, I honor you, I want to see you thrive." Here, amid the clang of pots and the fragrance of spices, we are reminded that to nourish is to love and to feed is to fortify the bonds that tether us together through the leanest times.

In this shared culinary journey, we are called to navigate the waters of personal preference and communal well-being, to find a balance between the taste of tradition and the promise of healthful living. It is a journey marked not by deprivation but by discovery — of new textures, new tastes, and the shared joy of exploration and evolution that makes the act of eating together an ever-unfolding adventure.

With hearts full and hands joined, we turn from the warming glow of a shared meal to the gentle embrace of mindful presence. In the next whispers of our journey, we learn to infuse our every day with the meditative calm of mindfulness, ensuring that the chaos of the world beyond our home does not overwhelm the peace we've fostered within.

As our bodies thrive on the sustenance we provide them, so too does our bond deepen, nourished by the knowledge that in caring for each other's physical vessels, we honor the beloved spirits within.

Mindfulness Amidst the Mundane: Embracing Serenity in the Swirl of Everyday

Enriched by the shared bounty of our tables and the unity of our spirits, we turn our hearts to the ever-flowing river of the day-to-day. Within the whirlwind of obligations, the hum of duties that often overshadow our inner peace, we are called to infuse tranquility into the tapestry of our commotion. This calls for a mindful step, a deliberate pause, a deep breath that roots us in the now, allowing us to savor each moment as it blooms and fades, rich with life's fleeting beauty.

Together, we endeavor to find stillness within the motion, to listen intently to the soft murmur of our inner selves amid the clatter of the tangible. Here lies the call of mindfulness—a gentle beckon to dwell in the present, to cradle attentiveness, and to foster deep, unwavering connection with one another, nestling it amid the creases of daily life.

As we navigate this plane, we learn that mindfulness is not a distant peak to be scaled, but a series of small steps taken with intention and grace. It is a sacred rhythm shared between us, where the rush of daybreak does not steal the tenderness of our clasped hands, nor the quiet affirmation of a shared glance. We nurture this mindfulness like a seedling in the garden of our marriage, watering it with patience and warming it with the sunlight of our focused presence.

In mindful living, we do not escape life's tempests but choose to stand within them, to face the winds of discord with a soulful hush, a whispered truth that within us lies an unshakable calm. We step into each day with the knowledge that mindfulness is our sanctuary, a consecrated space we carry within, where the rush of hours loses its frenzy, and the simplest acts become consecrated rituals of our love.

The art of mindfulness becomes a dance we perform in unison, a shared rhythm that carries us through the symphony of our daily tasks. We find serenity embedded in the rituals of waking, in the melody of morning birds, and the rhythm of stirring spoons against coffee cups. Together, we weave each strand of our day with the threads of attentiveness, adorning the fabric of our lives with rich hues of awareness and appreciation.

It is the graceful acceptance of life's intricate pattern, where each thread is an opportunity to practice presence, to raise a chorus of gratitude for the humdrum and the heavenly alike. With every mindful act, we affirm the strength and centrality of our bond—a connection that thrives not despite the daily grind but because of the sacredness we find within it.

This shared cultivation of mindfulness becomes the bedrock upon which we build the cathedral of our joint health. It forms intimate accessibility to each other's nuanced worlds, inspiring conversations that draw us closer, understanding that builds embankments against the currents of strife.

So let us hold closely this practice of mindfulness, cherishing it as a vessel that bears us steadily over the rivers of ordinariness into the depth of our shared journey. And it is along this stream, flowing with the gentle currents of conscious presence, that we prepare to dive deeper. We begin to explore the profound tapestry that aligns the health of our bodies with the vast reaches of our spirits, weaving a union strong enough to embrace both the visible and the invisible in the sacred dance of life.

The Spiritual Dimensions of Health: Merging the Physical With the Divine

The sweet cadence of daily mindfulness, makes us embrace the soulful recognition that our health transcends the physical, echoing into the profound corridors of the spirit. Health is not solely woven from the corporeal threads of nutrition and exercise but is a rich tapestry that includes the vibrant silks of our spiritual beliefs, the delicate laces of our emotional well-being, and the sturdy canvas of our collective resilience.

Together, we embark on a journey that marries the rhythms of our beating hearts with the tender hymns of our souls, acknowledging that our physical well-being is a reflection of our spiritual tranquility. It is in this synthesis that we find a deeper meaning in the whisper of each heartbeat, in the strength of every breath—a symphony of existence that resounds with the sacredness of life itself.

As we explore the interplay between our health and spirituality, we trace the contours of a shared sanctuary where the divine meets the tangible. Our bodies become temples, sacred vessels that house the essence of who we are, and in caring for them, we honor the Creator who sculpted us from stardust and spirit. In the soft glow of this understanding, every shared meal is communion, every joint endeavor a shared act of worship, and every triumph over illness a testament to the enduring power of faith and love.

The dialogue between our health and our spirits is rich with the language of compassion and empathy. We discover that each act of self-care is an ode to the divine within, a melody that soothes our insecurities and amplifies our shared strength. We are reminded that nurturing our health is an expression of gratitude for the gift of life, an embracing of the legacy we are bound to leave, a sign of respect for the majesty of creation.

In the shared pursuit of holistic health, we bind our aspirations to the virtue of patience, understanding that the path to wellness—like the journey of love—is a marathon, not a sprint. We find solace in shared silence as much as in joyous laughter, for each is a balm to the soul, a necessary note in the harmonious score of a balanced life. We hold fast to the truth that in the stillness of our inner beings, the whisper of divine guidance can be found, gently steering us toward choices that serve both body and soul.

In this communion of health and spirituality, we are called to be intentional. Our choices are purposeful, deliberate, and infused with the understanding that each leaf of kale, each moment of rest, each earnest prayer, is a knot tying us to a legacy far greater than ourselves. Being intentional lights the way as we teach our children the values of self-care, instilling in them reverence for the vessels they've been granted.

Yet, even as we celebrate this interconnectedness, we brace against the winds of adversity with unyielding hope. Illness may breach our defenses, and fatigue may seek to fray our resolve, but together we stand, unwavering, galvanized by the belief that our spiritual fortitude can weather any storm. Our shared path becomes an affirmation that even amid struggle, we are more than flesh and blood—we are resilient spirits, capable of renewal and boundless compassion.

As we bask in the light of this sacred union of health and spirit, we prepare to weave yet another strand into our —the understanding that our financial stewardship is as much a part of this holistic well-being as the food we consume and the meditations we embrace. With this wisdom, we step forward, ready to explore the financial terrains of our union, ensuring that our physical sanctuary and spiritual fortitude are matched by a foundation of economic stability. It is here, on the fertile ground of mutual diligence and shared wisdom, that we plant the seeds for a future that thrives in prosperity and purpose, watered by love, and lit by the enduring flame of our collective ambition.

Lachele's Personal Story

In our journey with The Bliss Protocol, Kofie and I have come to truly appreciate how our spiritual growth intertwines with our physical health. It's become such an integral part of our shared spiritual path.

You know, there's something special about the way we connect when we're active together. We absolutely treasure our travel time, those walks we take around our neighborhood, and our visits to this lovely park nearby where we often find ourselves strolling around the pond. It's in these moments, whether we're listening to worship music, grooving to some inspirational jazz, or just enjoying the quiet while holding hands, that we really open up to each other about our dreams and what we hope for in life.

But you want to know something funny? One of our favorite spots to visit is actually Planet Fitness - yes, the gym! It's where Kofie and I first met, so it holds a special place in our hearts. Now, Kofie, bless him, he loves those long, intense workouts. Me? Well, let's just say I prefer to keep things a bit shorter. I always joke, "I'll drive myself so I can leave when I'm ready!" It gets a laugh out of Kofie every time.

But you know what? That's the beauty of our relationship. We've learned to accommodate each other's preferences while still maintaining that strong bond between us. It's not always about doing everything exactly the same way or for the same amount of time. It's about finding that balance where we can share experiences, support each other's health journey, and still honor our individual needs. That's what keeps our connection strong and our spirits aligned.

Financial Foundations: Weaving Prosperity into Our Collective Fabric

In the quilt of wedded bliss, the thread of financial health is interwoven with the fibers of physical strength and the embroidery of spiritual unity. It is a vital pattern that, when carefully stitched, holds the power to support and protect the harmony of our intertwined lifelines.

As dual stewards of our shared resources, we acknowledge the delicate balance required to nurture the garden of our financial well-being. Each budgeted dollar and invested dime become symbols of our commitment to the collective dream—a dream dappled with the light of stability, the shade of growth, and the colors of cultural pride.

We come to understand that prosperity is not measured by the weight of gold but by the trust and communication that flourish within the boundaries of shared goals. It is a covenant of partnership where joint decisions reflect the depth of our connection, each financial plan a testament to the respect we hold for our combined future.

In this realm, money is not merely a currency but a tool for crafting legacies—legacies of education, of home, of philanthropy, and of freedom. We educate ourselves, determined to break any chains of economic hardship that history may have placed upon our ancestors' wrists. Thus enlightened, we move forward, guiding each other through the intricacies of wealth management with the same soulful patience that we bring to our health and mindfulness practices.

Practicality and vision merge as we consider each investment, each savings account, and each fiscal decision. We recognize that attaining financial health is akin to nurturing the body—it requires consistent care, a balanced approach, and an unwavering eye on long-term vitality.

In these shared endeavors, small steps lead to grand vistas. The simple act of planning a family budgeting meeting transforms into a ritual of connection, as intimate as a prayer whispered at twilight. We build our financial literacy as one would a fortress, brick by brick, book by book, seminar by seminar, knowing it is both a shield against life's storms and a beacon for our children's future.

Yet, beyond the mechanics of numbers, we imbue our financial journey with the spiritual understanding that true abundance flows from a well of generosity and gratitude. We give, not merely from our wallets, but from the heart, sowing seeds of hope and benevolence into the fertile soil of our community.

As we engage with our finances, conscious of the interconnectedness between our wealth and the blossoming of our holistic well-being, we lay down the stepping stones toward a bright horizon. It is a horizon where physical health and well-being ripple outward, reverberating through the essence of our shared spirituality and echoing back as financial serenity.

And so, as one chapter of our journey nears its gentle cadence, we steady our gaze on the promise of what lies ahead. We stand at the threshold of affirming our commitment to sustaining the holistic symphony of our marriage. It is here, in the convergence of health, spirit, and abundance, that we prepare to craft an affirmation that will resonate through the halls of our united existence, a covenant to cherish and uphold the holistic harmony that cradles our union.

Covenant of Wholeness: The Sustained Pulse of Enthusiastic Purpose

Affirmation: *"I commit to my personal growth, self-care, and self-love practices, knowing that the health of our relationship begins with the well-being of everyone. By nurturing myself, I contribute to the strength and harmony of our bond."*

Within the sacred cocoon of companionship, we affirm the essence of our holistic harmony—a dance of synchronous vitality where body, spirit, and prosperity find accord. This covenant, a composition of earnest pledges, enshrines the shared rhythm of our lives within the unbreakable circle of commitment and mutual reverence.

We stand together, hands clasped, eyes gleaming with the shared knowledge that our path is illuminated by more than the moon and stars above—it is brightened by the internal glow of our collective well-being. Here, we vocalize an affirmation, a sacred echo that resonates across the valleys and peaks of our unified journey.

"I pledge," we begin, as voices rise and merge in a chorus of intention, "to honor our combined health, nurturing the body with the reverence of a temple, attending to its needs with the tender care applied to a beloved child."

"And I vow," the response breathes life into the covenant, "to ensure that our mindfulness and spiritual fortitude are as inseparable as the earth and sky, a harmony that bolsters us through trials and serenades us in triumph."

As the warmth of our shared utterances fills the air, we acknowledge that the wealth we seek is cultivated in the richness of our laughter, the depth of our conversations, and the fortitude of our promises. We affirm that our financial health is but one note in our symphony—a note that rings clear and true, fortifying our ability to face the future with grace and to nurture a legacy that echoes down the corridors of time.

Our words intertwine like the intertwining roots of an ancient tree, finding strength not just in individual persistence, but in the unity that comes from deeply entwined purposes. This shared resolve cradles our spirits, offering a steady foundation from which to soar to new heights of understanding and achievement.

"With tender care, we will cultivate a garden of financial wisdom," we affirm. "A garden that blossoms with fruits of diligence, where the seeds of knowledge are watered with the rains of patience, and the blooms of fiscal responsibility bask in the sunlight of mindful stewardship."

With this pledge, we elevate our financial consciousness, intertwining it with the fabric of our holistic health. Together, we navigate the rivers of monetary decisions with the same grace with which we traverse the streams of our emotional and physical well-being.

And just as we tend to our bodies and our spirits, we affirm that we shall tend to our wealth—not as a master to a servant, but as a gardener to a precious plot of land, with the understanding that true abundance is born of more than figures on a balance sheet. It is born of the harmonious coalescence of all aspects of well-being.

We reflect on the profound intertwining of health, wealth, and spirit that forms the enduring bond of our shared existence. We prepare ourselves for the journey ahead, where the guardianship of our hard-earned resources becomes a mindful practice, an extension of our holistic wellness.

The next rhythms in our marital symphony await us with the gentle promise of revelation and understanding. We step forward, carrying the light of our holistic harmony into the realm of conscious stewardship, where each decision reflects the sacred connection of our hearts and the aligned values of our union. Here, we find the courage to cultivate our financial landscape with the same love, intention, and wisdom that fortify every other corner of our shared life.

As we journey together in marriage, we affirm our commitment to each other's wellbeing, inspired by the prayerful wish from 3 John 1:2: "May you prosper and be in good health, just as your soul prospers." We pledge to nurture not only our spiritual health but also our physical and emotional well-being, ensuring our mutual growth and prosperity mirror the depth of our spiritual connection. In this union, every aspect of our lives is intertwined, fostering a comprehensive approach to our love and care for one another, as we aim to flourish together in all dimensions of life.

9

Cultivating Mindful Wealth Management

Planning Together

Bethune Graphics

Conscious Financial Stewardship Within the Union

PRINCIPLE: Financial prosperity flourishes in the garden of mindfulness; intertwining acumen with awareness cultivates a stable future.

BLISS PROTOCOL #11: Shared Vision Quest:

- **Scenario:** Misaligned future goals
- **Solution:** Joint dream-building
- **Implementation:** Planning sessions, goal-setting
- **Key Advice:** Create unified direction for the future

In the sanctum of marital unity, where hearts are entwined and dreams coalesce into a vibrant mosaic of shared aspirations, arises the dawn of a new era in financial stewardship—a dawn where the sun of mindfulness casts golden rays upon the paths of prosperity that lay before us. "That Marriage Lyfe" invites you to embark on a journey, one that transcends the mundane transactions and elevates your fiscal union to a harmonious ballet danced to the rhythm of conscious intent and mutual respect.

Within these pages lies not merely the mechanics of money management but the soulful symphony of mindful wealth—a symphony orchestrated with care and precision, where every note echoes the depth of your shared values, and every melody resonates with a commitment to a future woven from the threads of both financial acumen and spiritual alignment. Here, in this sacred confluence, we lay the foundation for not just sustaining but flourishing in the garden of matrimonial commerce where every seed of intention is nurtured into abundance.

As we turn the soil in this garden, we understand that our bounty is not merely to satisfy the hunger of the present but to provide for the banquet of our future together. For the couple that strides hand in hand, shielded by understanding and armed with the courage of vulnerability, there exists a profound promise—a promise of cultivating a financial landscape where the stress of discord finds no purchase and the harvest of tranquility grows ever plentiful.

This is the promise of Cultivating Mindful Wealth Management: to guide you through the midnight mists of economic uncertainty with a lantern of wisdom, to transform the stolid walls of financial challenges into steppingstones towards a fortress of security built with bricks of empathy and mortar of patience.

Here, in the embrace of Conscious Financial Stewardship Within the Union, we plant the seeds that will sprout into a towering tree under whose shade future generations will sit and revel in the stories of your foresight and unity.

Let this be the chapter that invites you to the table of fellowship, where the meal of monetary matters is partaken with grace and gratitude. Here, we break bread over capital conversations, sip from the goblet of growth, and savor the sweet dessert of shared success. Transforming Money Talks lay ahead, where instead of the cacophony of conflict, the dialogue is a duet—heartfelt and attuned to the harmony of your union's vision.

As we turn the page, beckoning you to probe deeper into the continuity of this narrative, we lead you to the shimmering oasis of serenity in the desert of financial uncertainty. Ours is a sanctuary where the oasis is not a mirage, but a real haven crafted with the clay of compassion and the water of wisdom. Together, we will navigate the dunes, never losing sight of the star that guides us—the star of our joint aspirations and unshakeable faith in what we can achieve together.

Beloved, as you prepare to step forth into the expanse of Ethical and Spiritual Alignment in Finances, carry with you the understanding that each decision dripping from the quill of your financial dealings is a verse in the poem of your legacy. The ink is the essence of your shared ethics, the parchment—is the story of your love. Each stroke is deliberate, each line a reaffirmation of the vows that bind you both in purpose and in spirit.

So, take my hand, dear reader, and let us prepare to march proudly into the chapters that unfold with the promise of transformation, each step resounding with the echo of our principle. In the union of hearts, the unity of minds, and the consciences that bind, together, we shall cultivate a wealth that transcends currency and is measured in the richness of a life lived in alignment with the deepest convictions of soul, spirit, and love everlasting.

Transforming Money Talks: Turning Tension into Triumph

In the warm embrace of union, where two souls convene to chart the course of life hand in hand, the topic of money often looms like a cloud on a sunlit horizon. It's a dance that, even in the best of unions, can trip the most graceful of steps. Yet, it is within this very dance that we find the cadence of connection, the rhythm of resolve, and the melody that sings of triumph over tension. Welcome to the changing power of money talks, where, together, we turn whispers of worry into anthems of accomplishment.

Imagine this: A sanctuary where discussions about finances are not a source of dread but of exploration and mutual discovery—an intimate conversation cocooned in the comfort of trust and shared vision.

Here, we grasp that true prosperity begins not with currency but with the currency of clarity and communication.

So, sit with me at the table of transparency, where we feast upon the open-hearted exchange of perspectives, fears, and desires.

As we break the bread of budgeting and share the wine of financial planning, let us do so with the understanding that these moments are more than transactions; they are transactions of the heart. We delve into the depths of our journeys, acknowledge the baggage of past woes carried like coins in the pocket, and with gentle hands, we unpack them. For through this shared ritual of revealing, we build a bridge of understanding that spans the chasm of monetary misunderstanding and aligns us with the possible.

This sacred dialogue, this coupling of ambitions and apprehensions, becomes an opportunity to weave a stronger bond—one thread of trust at a time. In this space, the echo of our ancestors' wisdom rings clear: Together, we are stronger than the sum of our bank accounts. Together, we craft a financial tapestry rich with the hues of hope and the patterns of partnership.

As we pour out our concerns into the communal cup of conversation, remember that every word spoken in kindness is an investment in our joint emotional account. As we align our fiscal aims with the pillars of our shared existence, we recognize that our goals are not solitary ambitions but the shared summary of our collective dreams.

So let us commit to this culture of candid communion, where every sentence becomes a step towards synchrony, and every paragraph we pen together is a pledge to the prosperity of our partnership. We shall move mountains, and transmute the fear of lack into the fortress of fiscal security, founded upon the bedrock of mutual respect and adorned with the jewels of joint aspirations.

As we turn the page, be heartened by the knowledge that this open book of our relationship holds no secrets between its lines. On the horizon, a day dawns where the storm clouds of uncertainty give way to the open sky of collaborative courage. Herein lies the path through the wilderness of financial ambiguities, where we walk arm in arm, guided by the light of a shared resolve.

For what lies ahead is a journey through ever-changing landscapes of economic climates, where together we shall navigate the undulating terrain of the Unexpected. It is a journey suffused with the wisdom of the past and the promise of a flourishing future, where each decision, and each shared dream waters the seeds of a stable tomorrow.

Let us, with clasped hands and aligned hearts, set forth on this path with the comforting knowledge that our unity is the compass that will lead us through the valleys and peaks. And as we travel onwards, know that this is our journey—a rich and textured odyssey, embroidered with the threads of trust, spoken in the language of love, and paved with the gold of collective mindfulness.

Navigating Financial Uncertainties Together: Building Resilience as One

Nestled at the core of every shared life journey is the inherent truth that the winds of change are as constant as the northern star. It is within the sanctified bonds of marriage where the unforeseen can be met with a fortress of joint resilience, a unified front that stands steadfast against the swirling sands of financial uncertainty. In this shared space, we light the beacon of collective foresight, illuminating the path of preparedness that we tread together.

Embarking on this path, hand in hand, we embrace the realities of life's fluctuations with a spirit not of fear, but of poised readiness. Let us take solace in the knowledge that through the ebbs and flows, our unity becomes the chalice from which we drink the waters of serenity. We remember the adage of our forebears, that challenges are but the blacksmith's forge, where the iron of our bond is tempered into the steel of determination.

As we navigate the rolling tides of economic ups and downs, let us anchor our ship of matrimony with the weighted truth that resilience is not born from the absence of challenges, but rather the embracing of them. Together, we stand at the helm, charting a course where each storm faced en masse becomes a lesson in the art of togetherness—strategizing, planning, and heralding in the dawn of triumphs yet to come.

Equipped with an arsenal of adaptability, we reframe the narrative of uncertainty into an epic tale of joint adventure. With grace, we adjust sails to the prevailing winds, nimbly turning obstacles into waypoints on our journey toward a legacy of wisdom and wealth. This, my beloved, is the financial ballet we dance—a pas de deux of precision where fluidity meets firm resolve.

It is in these very waters that our plans are evaluated, and our unity fortified. Conversations that once might have sown seeds of discord now cultivate a garden of understanding. From the soil of this garden blossoms the blossom of empathy—for it is in seeing through the eyes of the other that we craft a shared vision robust against life.

Hand in hand, gaze locked with the future's vast expanse, we celebrate our collective strength. Each stride forward is a testament to our audacity to hope and our courage to love, not just in times of plenty but in every shade of life's seasons. It is here, on the shared road of financial uncertainties, that our love story unfolds—rich, textured, and brilliantly resilient.

And as we journey forth, we bear in mind that each decision we make is a pebble thrown into the pond of tomorrow, its ripples touching the shores of our coming days. Thus, with patience, we lay the stepping stones of careful planning and mutual support, leading us towards a horizon aglow with the promise of shared success and continued growth.

So, let us step boldly yet thoughtfully into the morrow, arm in arm, hearts aligned with a conviction that transcends the ledger. For it is within this dance of numbers and dreams that we find our true rhythm—the syncopated heartbeat of a partnership that can weather any storm.

As we turn yet another page in our story, let us do so with the silent whisper of commitment in our ears—a commitment to foster a world where our finances reflect not just our livelihood, but our life's values. This is our pledge, our solemn vow, to one another and to the future we build—a future where ethical considerations and spiritual wisdom inform every choice, every step along our shared financial pilgrimage.

Ethical and Spiritual Alignment in Finances: Synergizing Values with Ventures

In this tapestry we weave, vibrant threads of shared convictions and spiritual beliefs to form the pattern that guides our fiscal voyage.

As we stand, hand in hand, under the vast canopy of the heavens, we are reminded of the covenant of our union, which not only binds our hearts but aligns our moral compasses in pursuit of purposeful prosperity. For our wealth is not merely in the abundance of our coffers but in the richness of souls walking in step with integrity.

In the garden of our joint existence, let us not lose sight of the seeds of intent we plant with every financial choice. Each transaction, each dollar spent, reflects the credo etched within, a silent sermon preached through the pulpit of our pocketbooks. It is in the tender ground of ethical and spiritual consistency that we find our true north, a guiding star for monetary movements that resonate with our deepest values.

We stand before the marketplace of life, not as mere consumers but as stewards of a legacy that transcends the temporal. Our investments are more than economic; they are endowments of hope, acts of faith sown in the soil of the society we wish to nurture. As we deliberate on where to allot our resources, let the kneading of our joined hands mold a future kneaded with fairness, embraced by communities, and uplifted by our collective human spirit.

Together, we trace the lineage of our dollars, ensuring their journey aligns with the righteous path we have vowed to journey upon. We ask, do these coins cast shadows or light upon the world? Do they feed the mouths of the hungry, clothe the bare, and instruct the child? For it is in these interrogations of the heart that we discover a wealth that fills far more than bank vaults—it fills the very essence of our shared humanity.

Within this sacred dance of numerations and narrations, we honor the whispers of our ancestors, who knew the worth of wealth well woven with wisdom. Let our financial discourse echo the reverence of the past, infusing every spreadsheet with the spirit of generations that danced before us. As we sculpt a legacy, let it be one sculpted with the chisels of charity, etched with the etchings of enlightenment, and polished with the cloth of compassion.

As stewards of a future not just for ourselves but for those who follow, we carve out a haven where love and money meet—not in opposition but in a harmonious embrace. Our shared economic endeavors become hallowed ground, where the integrity of our intentions blesses the fruit of our labor. It is in this union of ethics and economics that we build a fortress fortified by mutual trust and adorned with the jewels of just deeds.

Let us proceed with assured steps, drawing strength from the sanctuary of our shared aspirations. For it is in our unity of purpose that every financial decision becomes an opportunity to our dedication to a collective vision shimmering with divine intention. The echoes of our laughter and the cadence of our footsteps merge into a melody that resounds with the frequency of mindful abundance.

In contemplation of our financial tapestry, rich with the patterns of our united vision, we ready ourselves to thread the next chapter of our odyssey together—a chapter where legacy is not just left but lived. In our shared pursuit of prosperity, let us vividly envision the orchards heavy with the fruit of our collective efforts, the legacies left for the children of tomorrow, and let this vision guide our hands as we write the narrative of our financial fellowship.

Kofie's Personal Story

"I've come to realize just how crucial it is for couples to align their focus and commitments when it comes to financial strategies, goals, dreams, and objectives. Looking back, I remember the journey Lachele and I took to align our financial future.

It's funny how different we were at first. I was great at short-term savings, always putting away money for immediate goals. Lachele, on the other hand, was a wizard at long-term savings, always thinking about our future years down the line. This mismatched approach caused some bumps in the road early on.

While I was acing the short-term savings game, I struggled with long-term financial planning. Although Lachele was fantastic at planning for our distant future, she found it challenging to save for more immediate needs.

We quickly realized we needed to sync up our approaches. We had to find a way to blend my short-term savvy with Lachele's long-term vision to create a comprehensive financial strategy that would sustain our entire life together.

This alignment, we believe, is a cornerstone of a successful marriage's financial portfolio. We've integrated Biblical principles into our financial planning, carefully considering our spending habits, savings strategies, and future goals. This approach has helped us stay in harmony with our financial structure.

Since we've aligned our financial goals and adopted these strategies, our financial life together has flourished. We're more successful not just in managing our money, but in working together as a team towards our shared financial future. It's been a game-changer for us, reinforcing the importance of unity in all aspects of marriage, especially when it comes to finances."

Building a Joint Legacy of Prosperity: Cultivating Generational Wealth with Intentionality

As we journey upon this sacred path, let the echoes of our forebears' wisdom guide us toward constructing a legacy that transcends the boundaries of our own lives. With our hands entwined and our hearts in congruence, we lay down the bricks of a future that blossoms with the fruits of our labor, a verdant garden of prosperity for generations to inherit.

The seeds we plant today are the legacies we tend to tomorrow, watered with purpose, pruned with foresight, and harvested with love.

In this union, where dreams converge and destinies intertwine, our collective aspirations for wealth become a canvas for visionary artistry. We paint with broad strokes of financial literacy, coloring our world with investments that bear the hallmark of stability and the promise of growth. Our conversations about wealth are not whispered in the hush-hush tones of secrecy but sung aloud like a hymn, resonating with the melodies of shared goals and mutual empowerment.

This reservoir of wealth we envision is not a shallow pool, but a deep wellspring fed by streams of knowledge, disciplined saving, and judicious investing. In the tapestry of our financial planning, we weave the threads of education for our children, innovation for our community, and sustainability for our environment. Long-term financial goals are set not as distant stars, but as guiding lights which we navigate by, always adjusting our course with patience and persistence.

As we craft this legacy of prosperity, we embrace the wisdom of collective strategizing, pooling our talents like a quilt of many patterns, each piece an essential part of the greater design. We affirm that true wealth is rooted not just in monetary abundance but in the rich soil of compassion, nurtured by the waters of generosity and illuminated by the sunlight of grace. It is wealth that builds homes, instills values, and uplifts the weary—wealth that is felt in the spirit as much as it is seen in material gain.

Let us, therefore, wield our financial resources as tools for crafting a brighter future—one where ethical investment paves the roads, philanthropy lights the streetlamps, and the youth are the architects of their own destinies. In every financial strategy, we hear the ancestral drums beating a rhythm that calls us to invest as much in our heritage as we do in our hedge funds, ensuring that wealth is a vessel for communal awakening and spiritual revival.

It is with prudent hearts and sharp vision that we plot our journey toward this horizon of abundance. Our legacy is etched not only in the ledgers of banks but in the lines of poetry that our lives become—an anthology of effort, a chorus of triumph. In the unity of our fiscal endeavors, we find a strength that bears the weight of our dreams and a faith that lights the way for those who will walk this path after us.

As we come together, let our legacy be marked by the footprints we leave in the sands of time—foot stamps that others may follow toward their own summits of success. In this dance of numbers and narratives, we choreograph a routine of responsibility, an ode to the future we are shaping with every choice, every sacrifice, and every victory in our pursuit of prosperity.

Our shared journey of wealth accumulation is thus a pilgrimage towards a promised land of bounty—a land where the dreams we plant today become the realities we live tomorrow. This shared vision of our future is a sacred covenant, each day renewed, each night reflecting the stars of possibility. Let our evolving story be a testament to the unyielding power of love, unity, and mindful wealth management.

And as we look toward the landscape ahead, brimming with potential and promise, let us move forward with courage and intention, knowing that the path we carve will be filled with the milestones of our dedication—a dedication to a legacy that blooms with abundance, and a life's work that stands as a beacon of inspiration, guiding us into the celebration of each achievement along the way.

Celebrating Financial Milestones: Savoring the Fruits of Collaborative Fiscal Harmony

In the symphony of our unified financial journey, each milestone is a note that resonates with the harmony of our collective efforts. These markers deserve recognition—for each one is a testament to our fortitude, an embodiment of shared dreams metamorphosed into tangible triumphs. As we traverse the path of building a joint legacy, it is vital to pause, acknowledge, and celebrate the victories, both small and grand, in our dance of financial alignment.

Together, in the glow of newfound achievements, we gather the bouquets of our diligence. It may be the jubilation of a debt extinguished, the quiet pride of a goal reached, the serene satisfaction of a nest egg that grows beneath the warmth of our prudent planning. Each success is a brush stroke on the masterpiece of our lives together, colors blending in the majesty of mutual accord and effort.

Acknowledgement should be as intentional as our investments, for the act of celebration is a balm to the soul, a well-deserved respite that fortifies us for the road ahead. These are moments etched in the annals of our story, shared over dinner tables and before the light of firesides, where we recount the journey thus far with gentle laughter and reflective joy.

To savor the fruits is not merely to revel in the result but to cherish the journey—the planning, the saving, the choices, and the sacrifices that are the invisible roots of visible prosperity. It is a collective toast to resilience; a nod to the foresight that bore the fruit; a hug for the patience that nurtured the dream into fruition. For those we love, these celebrations become the lore of our legacy, a narrative of triumph laced with lessons and love.

In these shared experiences of celebration, we are weaving a tapestry of memories that, like a quilt, warms future generations. We instill in our kin the value that wealth is not defined by abundance alone but also by the capacity to appreciate and share the journey it has afforded us. Our joy becomes a beacon that lights the way for others, illuminating the road of possibilities, and encouraging others to embark on their own voyages of financial enlightenment.

And as we clink our glasses and carve our milestones into the grand oak of our shared history, we are reminded of the strength within our unity. Triumph is not the echo of a solitary cheer but the chorus of a family in jubilee, celebrating not just the realization of financial goals but the bond that made such achievements possible.

Let the festivities inspire us to aim for even loftier peaks. Let every congratulatory word, every encouraging embrace embolden us to dream with boundless optimism. Through every season of abundance and each cycle of challenge, our journey is a lesson in the art of gratitude and the craft of celebration.

The vibrance of these moments carries us forward, into the genesis of tomorrow's aspirations. Our shared victory song becomes the prelude to the dawn of new commitments and the setting forth on continued quests. In these celebratory echoes, we find the strength to wield our collective purpose and to paint our future with strokes of gratitude, love, and unending hope.

Affirmation of Financial Unity and Mindfulness: Embracing Our Collective Journey with Intention

Affirmation: *"We develop meaningful daily, weekly, and seasonal rituals that bring us together and reaffirm our bond. Through morning check-ins, weekly dates, and annual recommitment ceremonies, we celebrate our love and strengthen our connection."*

As we stand together, looking back with gratitude at the milestones we've celebrated, our hearts swell with a renewed sense of unity. The essence of our journey is not captured merely by the figures in our bank accounts, but by the strength of our bond and our unwavering commitment to walk this path together. We affirm in this moment our shared conviction in mindful wealth management—an understanding that every penny saved, every investment made, reflects our collective vision and the deep-rooted values that unite us.

With wisdom as our compass and intention as our guide, we navigate the waters of fiscal responsibility—not as an act of solitary duty, but as a profound expression of mutual love and care. It is through the lens of mindfulness that we discern the true worth of our financial decisions, for they serve as stones paving the way to a future of abundance, security, and shared joy.

We take this time to affirm, with hope and determination, our pledge to uphold the sanctity of our financial stewardship. In the tapestry of our united story, each thread represents a choice, each color a decision that shapes the legacy we aspire to leave behind. We weave our commitments with steady hands, ever mindful of the fabric we create together—a fabric that shelters, nurtures, and honors the essence of our partnership

.

Let our affirmation resonate beyond the echoes of words spoken; let it manifest in the actions we take each day. Let our shared financial endeavors be ever intentional, blessed by a spirit of cooperation and graced with an unobstructed vision for the future. In this declaration, we embrace the beauty of synchronicity, celebrating not only our togetherness but the soulful journey we share.

In acknowledging our unity, we find strength in the diversity of our experiences, courage in the face of adversity, and wisdom in the lessons learned. We treasure the communal spirit of this journey, understanding that while we may hold the pen that writes our financial legacy, it is the shared ink that flows, rich with the hues of trust, respect, and unwavering support.

As we prepare ourselves for the footsteps yet to take, may each stride carry with it the affirmation of our purpose and the depth of our connection. With clear eyes, we glimpse the horizon anew, recognizing the boundless potential that awaits us. Our affirmation is not a solitary promise but a harmonic chorus—a song that uplifts, unites, and propels us toward the dawn of a prosperous tomorrow.

It is with this resonant melody in our hearts that we step forward, ready to encounter the spaces where our financial mindfulness and community spirit converge. Together, we embrace the next chapter, where the warmth of collective joy and social synergy beckons us to connect, to share, and to enrich not only our own lives but the fabric of the community we treasure. With open hearts, we move into a space where the magnificence of love and togetherness becomes the cornerstone of every encounter, every shared effort, and every triumph we celebrate together.

10
Cultivating Collective Joy

Cultivating Joy and Community
Bethune Graphics

Social Synergy and Community Connection

PRINCIPLE: "Collective joy is the tapestry of shared experiences; woven with threads of community and friendship, it enriches the soul and strengthens bonds."

BLISS PROTOCOL #7: Shared Adventures:

- **Scenario:** Relationship monotony
- **Solution:** New experiences together
- **Implementation:** Adventure planning
- **Key Advice:** Break routine with novelty

Beneath the quilt of stars that stretch across the vastness of night, we find the constellation of human connection—a pattern of interwoven lives and shared moments illustrating the grand design of our existence. It is within this intricacy of relationship that the principle of collective joy emerges, binding us with invisible yet unbreakable threads—a warm covering of our own making, adorned with the colors of our community and the textures of our friendships.

To embark upon this journey of collective joy is to declare that the harmonic convergence of two hearts is but the prelude to greater symphonies; symphonies that resonate with the laughter of companions, the support of acquaintances, and the compassion of strangers. Harmony in matrimony, much like the delicate interplay of instruments in an orchestra, requires not only the melody of passion but the accompaniment of a broader familial chorus—a community that dances to the rhythm of shared purpose and joined destinies.

In this chapter, we honor the commitment of couples to stoke the fires of joy not just within the sanctum of intimacy, but within the broader arena of societal engagement. We acknowledge the truth that joy shared is joy amplified, and that the roots of happiness thrive in the rich soil of mutual experiences and collective endeavors.

We rise to the clarion call to bind our lives together with more than vows—building bridges between our personal isles and the mainland of our communities. From the sanctity of love's embrace, the promise made is this: to transcend boundaries, to reach out and enmesh in the network of relationships that constitutes the lifeline of a society.

In doing so, we breathe new life into not only our relationships but also into the very essence of our towns, our cities, and our nations.

Allow this chapter to be a compass that guides you towards the untapped reservoirs of joy within your union, pointing towards the horizons of social endeavors, community service, and common passions that await your discovery. Together, you will explore the landscapes of love that stretch beyond the privacy of shared whispers and into the public squares of collective action and mutual support.

As the dawn illuminates the path before us, let us step boldly into this journey, hand in hand, heart to heart, with the spirits of our ancestors marching beside us—a chorus of wisdom and strength cheering us onward. With each chapter of our lives unfurling like the petals of a rose greeting the sun, we find the beauty in the kaleidoscope of human interaction, the strength in unity, and the breathtaking power of cultivating collective joy.

Embrace this chapter as you would a dear friend, let it lead you through the garden of community where every seed sown with love blossoms into a flower of joy. For within these pages lies not only the promise of joy but the roadmap to a life where every shared smile and every act of kindness is a stroke on the canvas of your love story—a masterpiece in the making.

Weaving Social Tapestries Together

The rich hues and intricate patterns of a tapestry do not emerge from a single thread, but from the multitude of strands expertly woven together, each contributing its unique shade and texture to the overall design. Similarly, the fabric of our relationships are woven from the various threads of our individual lives—friends met along divergent paths, family ties that bind, and casual acquaintances who, at times, provide unexpected bursts of color.

In the dance of matrimony, as in the rhythm of an age-old spiritual, there is both a solo and a collective performance. It is the art of weaving these threads—yours, mine, ours—into a cohesive whole that we accept the delicate, yet critical challenge in this stage of our shared journey. The artistry comes in knowing that while some threads may initially seem disparate, it is through the intentional act of weaving them together that a larger, shared network of social support is created.

Couples sometimes struggle to blend their individual social spheres, each rich with history and memories. To merge these separate spheres requires an understanding that the mosaic of our past experiences can, and should, enhance the present unity. Embrace the opportunity to broaden your shared sphere, allowing the lure of past connections to create a dance floor large enough for two.

Imagine each friendship as an invitation to a grand ball, a celebration of cultures and voices harmonizing to create a melody uniquely yours. Introduce the joys of your partner's world to your own, crafting a social rhythm that moves effortlessly between the old and the new, the familiar and the yet-to-be-discovered. Together, step into the embrace of this shared circle with confidence, knowing that as you do, the combined strength of your relationships will echo the depth of your love.

Community is not merely a backdrop to our lives but is central to the narrative we create together. It imparts lessons that only collective experiences can teach—empathy, diversity, and acceptance. It is in these moments of coming together, of gathering around tables graced with laughter and stories, that the collage of humanity touches our hearts.

As we gather at these tables, side by side, allow this communal feast to nourish not only our bodies but our spirits as well. For in each shared glance, every resonant chuckle lies an affirmation that our union is not a fortress against the world, but an open home, inviting and vibrant. We become architects of a social sanctuary where every guest becomes part of the foundation, every interaction a brick laid with love and intention.

It is important to remember that the gift of friendship is reciprocal; to receive, we must also be willing to give. Extend an invitation, be a gracious host, and let the warmth of genuine connection guide the way as new friendships bloom—bearing fruit in the gardens of your shared existence.

Let the pages here be the roadmap to a place where friends old and new sit at the same table, sharing in the feast of joy that life offers. This convergence is not just a meeting point but a crossroad of destinies where the legacy of camaraderie becomes as significant as the bonds you've pledged to each other.

As this tapestry continues to unfold, we find that the delicate balance of weaving our social networks is not a journey we take alone. It is a shared expedition, abounding with opportunities to knit together a collective embrace that shelters and sustains our love. From this place of interconnection, we discover the blessings that lie in the multitude, the stories etched in the faces of friends, and the love that grows in the laughter and unity of the community.

With this understanding, we turn our gaze to that which lies ahead—a horizon filled with possibilities as we explore the balance between the intimacy we cherish and the wider world that awaits our touch.

Balancing Intimacy with Social Expansion

Somewhere in the sacred dance between the silences that define our intimacy and the crescendo of voices that comprise our social circles, lies a delicate rhythm—a balance sought by hearts that beat both for solitude with one's love and for the fellowship with the community. It is here, within this tender balance, that we find the space to grow together, even as we expand our embrace to include the world beyond our doorstep.

In the quiet moments we share, whispered secrets and tender gazes weave a silken cocoon that nurtures our bond, providing a sanctuary of peace and solace. This is the private garden where our love grows, tended, and cherished; but just beyond the garden's gate is a vast landscape aglow with the light of innumerable connections—a tapestry of human experience waiting to be explored.

As we stand hand in hand, our toes brushing against the threshold between the intimacy we have nurtured and the community that beckons, we must step forward with intention. We move in concert with the understanding that while our love is the nucleus of our world, the orbit of our lives can, and should, encompass the myriad stars that populate our social universe.

The warmth of shared smiles at a community gathering, the invigorating exchange of ideas in a group setting, and the collective hum of a shared purpose—these are but a few of the experiences that enliven the fabric of our relationships. To engage in such social spheres while safeguarding the sanctity of our intimate moments requires vigilance and wisdom. It necessitates an ongoing conversation, a delicate negotiation of time and energy so that neither the quiet sanctuary of our union nor the ebullient company of our friends outweighs the other.

Carefully, we must allocate the hours of our days, ensuring that the depth of our private communion is not lost in a sea of external demands. We must wear the garment of balance—a robe woven with threads of both seclusion and solidarity. Just as a choir's beauty is found in the sum of its voices, each perfectly pitched and timed, so too is the beauty of our life's chorus found in the harmony between our private and public lives.

As we delve into the heart space of our community, let us carry with us the lessons learned in the soft hush of our togetherness. In the give and take of conversation, in the laughter shared over meals, in the shared goals and aspirations with others, we become reflections of each other—mirrors amplifying the best within us.

Yet never shall we forget that true balance is a dance that requires continuous adjustment, a step back for every leap forward. With every social stride we take, let us glance backward, ensuring that our partner's hand is still firmly grasped in ours and that the compass of our journey remains true to the sacred space we've cultivated at home.

Here, in the interstitial spaces between 'us' and 'them', we find that balance is less a destination and more an act of constant navigation—an ebb and flow of presence and togetherness that elevates all aspects of our existence. It is an endeavor not devoid of challenge, but rich with the potential for growth and boundless joy.

As we move gently through the pages of this chapter, let them be a reminder that the pursuit of balance is a testament to the strength of our commitment, not just to each other, but to the broader canvas of life that we paint with every shared memory and collective experience. It is with this understanding that we now turn our hearts towards a journey of unity, seeking the threads that bind us in common cause and shared passion, as we continue to paint the masterpiece of our life together.

United by Cause: Finding Shared Passions

In the tapestry of marriage, each thread represents a unique passion, hobby, or cause that adds vibrancy and strength to the woven whole. As couples stride forward on the path of togetherness, the quest becomes discovering these harmonious threads that bind their spirits in shared purpose—those activities that resonate within the hearts of both, igniting a fire of joint enthusiasm and unified endeavor.

This discovery, this seeking of common ground, is not merely about juggling each other's interests, but rather about the cultivation of a fertile ground where the seeds of new passions may take root—where individual desires merge to form a collective dream. It is here, in the willingness to embark upon a journey of combined exploration, that the true magic of unity blossoms.

Together, you might find yourselves drawn to the ancient art of gardening, your hands coated in the earth that symbolizes the nurturing of life—yours and that which you plant. Or it is through the melodies of music, whether strumming strings or harmonizing voices, that you find your shared heartbeat. It could be the brushstrokes of art, the twist of a dance, or the rippling effect of community service that brings to life the shared passions of your duet.

It is through these endeavors, diverse and enriched by common intention, that we start to see the reflection of our deeper selves. The principles of our faith, resilience against challenges, the wisdom gleaned from our ancestors—all come together in the activities we choose to take on together. When we find a cause that stirs both souls, it is as though a symphony resounds with each step we take, each decision to give back, to learn, to create.

Imagine the impact when two become one in pursuit of philanthropy, and how the actions of united lovers can uplift a community. Envision the joy cultivated through mentoring the young, through sharing your journey's experiences with those who have just begun to wade into life's currents. To impart knowledge, to empower others—this too, is a shared passion that not only enriches the lives of others but cements your legacy as a couple who transcends the individual.

Some may discover that their shared quest leads them to the halls of advocacy, where together they raise their voices for justice and equity, embodying the spirit of those who marched and dreamed before them. Others may find solace in the peace of spiritual retreats or a dedication to health and fitness, aligning mind, body, and soul in the pursuit of holistic wellness.

These shared pursuits are pearls strung together, creating a necklace of shared existence that adorns the relationship with purpose and intentionality. Each pursuit is a thread in the bond, each cause, a chapter in the story you write with united pens.

Let the rhythm of exploring shared passions be like a gentle river that carves its way through the landscape of your life, shaping and nourishing the earth it touches. Embrace the possibilities that unfold when we open our hearts to the potential treasures buried within our partner's passions and our own.

As we draw each chapter to a close, the story flows naturally forward—each revelation of shared interest, each success in community action, becomes a stepping stone to the next adventure. It is within this continuous flow of discovery, this embrace of shared initiatives, that we find ourselves cultivating a garden of everlasting impact, nourishing our spirits and the life we lead side by side. And it is with this nourishment that we turn our attention to the next chapter in our journey—the celebrations and tributes that come from giving back to the communities that hold us together.

We found that once our Destinies collided and we became lifelong Destiny partners we realized that our individual calls from God aligned together next we had to identify what Passions each other had and what convictions we share and then collaborate on how to join together in doing what we felt God called us to do individually to now be collectively and now we are in Ministry together saving Souls together perfecting the Saints together strengthening women together strengthening men together fortifying families together all because we decided to step into our destiny and to create Legacy with each other.

Celebrating Community: The Joy of Giving Back

Within the boundless realm of love, there is wealth—a treasure not hoarded but shared, a cornucopia that multiplies as it is given freely. The act of giving back to the community, of planting seeds of benevolence that bear the fruit of collective betterment, this is where the symphony of shared life crescendos into a melody that echoes far beyond the walls of a home. It is within the embrace of giving that couples discover an expanding universe of joy—a joy that is cultivated together and radiates outward.

To give back, to serve, to extend the quilt of care to encompass all who shiver—this is an intimate dance celebrated in the wider halls of humanity. The shared commitment to volunteering, to rolling up sleeves beside one former stranger who becomes part of an extended family, enhances the filament that connects one heart to another. It is this very act of service that forges a stronger union, as partners witness each other in the light of altruism, in spaces where love becomes a verb actively lived aloud.

Communities flourish when hearts join in service when the strength of two backs bending to uplift others is witnessed; it is in these moments that the true power of a unified vision is palpable. It might be through nourishment provided at a local food bank, in the spark of knowledge ignited by tutoring children, or in the comfort of companionship offered at a senior center, that you find the reflection of your joint highest selves—giving without the expectation of receiving.

Such shared activities, these altruistic endeavors, function as the soil from which appreciation and admiration for one another grow. As you serve alongside one another, you are not merely partners; you are champions of a cause greater than yourselves, unified by a purpose that ignites a blaze of compassion and camaraderie.

As you become inhabitants of a world built on generosity, you bear witness to the transformation that springs from the smallest of seeds. You see the smiles that blossom from the nourishment of both body and soul, the gratitude that springs forth like a well from parched ground. In each of these moments, you recognize a truth as old as time—that in giving, we receive, and there is no greater joy than the joy discovered in service to one another.

Imagine, then, the celebrations that come alive when a community gathers, not just to receive but to recognize and honor each other's contributions. These celebrations become milestones; markers of the journey walked hand in hand. They become legends told in the laughter of elders, the ballads of youth, and the murmur of everyday folk—stories that will be woven into the tapestry of your shared history.

Dressing in the raiment of generosity, let us then find our way to the hearth where memories are shared, and bonds are strengthened, not only within the protective embrace of our arms but within the wider circle of our community. Let this rhythm of giving back, this cycle of service, be a pilgrimage we embark upon with hearts wide open, discovering new landscapes of joy with every step we tread.

Thus, our narrative dances forward, flowing into new rivers of discovery, where the simple brilliance of shared hobbies and interests can ignite a constellation of joy in the night sky of life's journey. Here, in the fertile grounds of service, let us plant the seeds of passion and watch them grow into bountiful gardens where love, laughter, and the fruits of community labor are enjoyed by all.

Cultivating Joy in Shared Hobbies and Interests

In the tapestry of life, each thread interwoven with another creates a pattern rich with the colors of experience. As we navigate the terrain of togetherness, discovering shared hobbies and interests becomes a sacred act—a pilgrimage toward joy where each shared activity becomes a stepping stone to a deeper connection. When two souls embark on a journey to explore the vast landscapes of their individual and collective curiosity, they create a shared storyline that resonates with the laughter of discovery and the warmth of companionship.

This exploration is a garden where the fruits of mutual interests are ripe for picking. It is in these shared spaces that couples may find themselves shoulder to shoulder, painting on the same canvas of existence. Be it the culinary arts, where the kitchen becomes an altar of creativity and flavors blend not only in the pots and pans but in the essence of shared achievement. Or it's found in the simple, quiet joy of reading side by side, where words become the vehicles transporting you both to places of profound understanding and reflection.

The act of engaging together in hobbies and interests acts as a lighthouse, guiding couples to shores alight with new possibilities. For some, the rhythmic cadence of a shared athletic pursuit offers more than just the rush of adrenaline—it becomes a metaphor for support, for the enduring nature of encouragement as one may guide or cheer the other crossing their proverbial finish lines. For others, the pursuit may lie in artistic expression, where music, painting, or writing becomes a duet—a song of two hearts that beats to the drum of mutual passion.

Every shared endeavor opens the door to a new room within the heart, a chamber filled with the echoes of joy that only harmony of purpose can bring. It's in these moments of collaboration and shared interest that the bond is nurtured and the relationship is steeped in the richness of shared passions. The laughter that bubbles up when an unfamiliar dance step is mastered, the pride that swells when a joint project is completed—each is a testament to the sweetness of togetherness.

The fabric of shared joy is not solely woven in the grandiose or the extravagant. Often, it's found in the nuanced stitches of the day-to-day—planting a garden, curating a collection, or even the serenity of bird watching can become sanctuaries of shared delight. These are the realms where love doesn't just whisper; it sings in clear, resonant tones, each note a vow to pursue that which ignites the couple's spirit.

In cultivating these shared interests, we nurture the soil from which empathy and understanding sprout. When we immerse ourselves in the world of our beloved, we see through their eyes, feel with their hearts, and learn the cadence of their inner song. And it is within this learning that fortifies as much as it delights, that any discord gives way to the sweet harmony of shared experience.

Let us not forget that it is through the windows of these activities that the soul peers out, offering a gaze into the landscape where the spirit plays. And as we explore hand in hand, the foundation laid by giving back to our community grounds us in these new pursuits, these new worlds of joy we build not apart but amidst the truest connection of all.

Therein lies the prelude to an ever-deepening love, to a journey towards the affirmation of our social and community connections. Like a river that meets the ocean, our individual passions converge into an expansive sea of shared joy, setting the stage for a vow—an affirmation not merely spoken but lived, a pledge to continue nurturing the bridge between soulful togetherness and the enrichment of the world we share.

Affirmation of Social and Community Connection

Affirmation: "*We embrace shared adventures, breaking free from routines and complacency by exploring new experiences, hobbies, and adventures together. Through novelty, play, and shared passion, we continually infuse our relationship with excitement and joy.*"

With the resonant hum of attuned hearts and hands enlaced in shared purpose, we arrive upon a clearing – a space of affirmation where the sacred echoes of collective joy harmonize with the melody of social and community connection. Here, love is not merely a personal sanctuary, but a beacon that shines outward, illuminating the path for others as they navigate the complexities and the beauty of togetherness.

This affirmation stands as a testament to the garden we've cultivated together, where laughter has watered the earth and our shared passions have taken root, flourishing into a beautiful ecosystem of togetherness. From the tapestry of threaded experiences in community service to the songs serenaded in the key common interests, this affirmation is our promise to never cease in our endeavor to intertwine our souls not just with each other, but with the world around us.

With hands clasped and eyes gazing into the horizon of our future, we affirm our commitment to foster a togetherness that transcends the physical – one that crafts a network of souls, bound by the joy of shared experiences and the strength found in the assembly of our communal spirit. We are not islands adrift but rather co-creators of a bridge that connects the archipelagos of our individualities to the mainland of unity.

In every shared silence, in the collective energy of a community event, in the mirrored passion for a hobby, there is the soft whisper of this affirmation, resounding through the fibers of our being: We vow to continue investing in the richness of our shared life, to elevate it with the contributions of those we meet along the path, and to celebrate every triumph as a collective victory.

It is within this affirmation that we recognize the truth – our connections extend beyond the confines of our abode, into the social circles that we nurture and the communities that we serve. They are the lifeblood that carries the essence of our kinship, pulsating with the vibrant hues of cultural richness, emotional courage, and a spirituality that transcends the physical plane.

Our journey together is both a triumph and a testimony, an ode to the resilience that radiates from a love carefully curated and steeped in a legacy of shared endeavor. So, as we stand firmly rooted in our present, our eyes locked in unwavering gaze upon the landscape of our collective flourishing, we embrace the kinship of every kindred spirit we encounter. With them, we build more than a fleeting chorus; we compose an everlasting symphony that will be etched in the annals of our shared history.

As we move from the garden of our hobbies and interests, we prepare for a new dawn. With the fertile soil beneath our feet, which has borne the fruits of joy and woven the threads of lasting memories, we step forward. There, on the horizon, the promise of expanding love lies within the trustworthy embrace of kindred spirits and allies. This is the circle of trust, where the boundaries of support and mutual growth stretch wide, embracing us all in an unending cycle of care and empowerment.

For it is in the fellowship of souls that the true power of life's shared journey becomes evident, and in the tapestry of relationships – nurtured, treasured, and tended to – that we ultimately find the strength to ascend to greater heights, side by side, anchored in love and propelled by a collective vision of a life well-lived and an existence that reverberates with deep, resonant joy.

11

Expanding the Circle of Trust

Expanding the Circle of Trust

Bethune Graphics

Cultivating Trusted Networks for Mutual Support

PRINCIPLE: "Trust weaves the fabric of communal bonds; expanding our circle invites a tapestry of support and shared joy."

BLISS PROTOCOL #3: Vulnerability and Authenticity:

- **Scenario:** Emotional walls and barriers
- **Solution:** Creating a safe space for sharing
- **Implementation:** Trust-building exercises
- **Key Advice:** Open sharing of feelings and fears

In the sanctum of our hearts, in the warm embrace of kindred spirits—this is where trust thrives, a gentle yet unyielding strength that binds us to one another. Trust is not merely the cornerstone of love between two souls but the expansive foundation upon which entire communities are built. As we undertake the sacred endeavor of matrimony, we are called upon to merge worlds, to blend the vivid tapestries of our individual lives into a masterpiece of mutual support and interwoven destinies.

The journey of marriage, like the flow of a majestic river, brings forth the confluence of two streams, each enriched by its unique tributaries of friendship, tradition, and experience. Embracing this flow, we find ourselves wrapped in the principle that trust weaves the fabric of communal bonds, where expanding our circle invites a tapestry of support and shared joy. This passage we embark upon does not ask us to forsake the cherished connections of days gone by but invites us to cultivate a garden where the blooms of old friendships and the seeds of new ties flourish side by side.

Binding the solitary strands of our lives, trust in union becomes the loom on which we weave our shared future. It is in the laughter that bounces through the walls of family gatherings, the understanding nods exchanged in times of tribulation, and the symphony of voices raised in the celebration that the melody of this trust is composed. Recognizing this, we shall explore how to bring together the separate worlds that have molded us, honoring individuality while forging a shared identity within our wider circle.

Our passage through this chapter will be akin to navigating the steps of a grand ballroom dance—a journey of rhythm and grace, of intricate footsteps leading towards synchronicity. Here, we will learn the art of harmonizing the precious private realm of matrimonial intimacy with the joyous clatter of social engagement. We shall discover the euphony that rises when our spirits find a common cadence in causes and purposes that resonate with our shared consciousness.

In unity, we are more than just two—we become a part of something larger, a circle extending its embrace to encompass friends, family, neighbors, and beyond. We shall uncover the delicate threads that weave together a supportive network, each connection an opportunity to enhance our shared lives. These are not mere idle acquaintances but trusted allies in the dance of life, companions in whom we find strength, solace, and celebration.

As we traverse the pages of this chapter, let us invite wisdom to guide our steps and love to light the way. The promise for you, dear reader, is a blueprint for crafting a circle of trust that transcends the solitude of individual paths, creating a community chorus that elevates the sacred duet of marriage. It is a journey of growth, understanding, and profound transformation—a transformation that we foreshadow here with the eager anticipation of the blessings yet to unfold.

As we embrace this invigorating exploration, bear witness to the mosaic of life, the interplay of connection, and the power of trust radiating through the very soul of the community. It is here, in this celebration of unity, that we shall discover how the cycle of giving and receiving fortifies the spirit and buoys the heart. Let us proceed, hand in hand, stepping boldly into the inviting embrace of a world eager for the warmth of our expansive trust.

With hope blooming in every word, we turn now to the merging of worlds and the artful tapestry of integrating separate social lives into a cohesive, shared existence.

Merging Worlds: Integrating Separate Social Lives

The dance of life, rich with the movement and rhythm of relationships, beckons us to weave our individual threads into a shared tapestry that strengthens the bond between us. As partners in the profound concert of matrimony, the challenge before us is akin to a maestro conducting harmonies from distinct musicians, creating a symphony that celebrates both the individual and the collective. In this melody of life, each partner brings a unique repertoire of friendships, kindred souls who have journeyed alongside them, enriching their existence.

To merge these separate social spheres is to embark on an odyssey of integration, one that cherishes the sacred space of togetherness while honoring the distinct echoes of our personal histories. The goal is not to dissolve the identity that has been crafted through years of individual experiences, but rather to blend these vibrant colors into a masterpiece that pays homage to both the singular and the united path.

The act of merging worlds begins with an open embrace, an invitation extended to each other's cherished companions, acknowledging their roles in our partner's life narratives. It calls for thoughtful conversations that breathe life into shared interests and mutual acquaintances, fortifying the foundation of our relationships with an understanding that compassionately acknowledges each soul's story.

In this process, we uncover the delight of new connections—a friend of a spouse who becomes a trusted confidant, a colleague who transitions to a family friend, and neighbors who transform into pillars of our expanded community. These connections, once solitary stars in our partner's constellations, begin to form new constellations that illuminate our shared night sky.

Constructing this bridge between worlds necessitates focus. It's about creating spaces for these intersections to occur—dinners that turn strangers into friends, gatherings where laughter is the currency of bonding, and shared experiences that become the fertile soil for trust to flourish. It is a loving art, the crafting together of disparate lives into a collective narrative that holds the weight of shared histories and future dreams.

We also realize that as we open our worlds to each other, friction may arise—a natural part of the human canvas. But it is through navigating these moments with grace, empathy, and a spirit of conciliation that our shared circles grow stronger. These are not stumbling blocks but stepping stones, each one paving the way to a richer, more inclusive world.

Recall the joy that comes from discovering a shared love for the soul-stirring rhythms of jazz or the kindred passion for morning runs as the sun kisses the horizon. The introduction of our partner's acquaintances can lead to a fusion of passions, a blending of melodies that resonates with the deeper parts of our being, evoking new harmonies within the orchestra of our lives.

As we turn the page, let us carry forth the intention to continue nurturing the gardens of our relationships with steady hands and open hearts. Let the beauty of these merging worlds unfold, as the roots of old trees intertwine with new saplings—each adding their strength, their stories, their essence to the soil of our collective experience. This act of integration is but the prelude to the resplendent harmony that awaits, a harmony that balances the sweet intimacy of partnership with the vibrant chords of our social symphony.

Harmony Between Intimacy and Social Engagement

In the delicate waltz of marriage, where hearts move to the rhythm of unity and spirits sync in tender embrace, there lies the dance floor of life, where intimacy meets society, where the private cocoon of love extends into the vast garden of community. Here, in this sacred space, the beautiful dance of harmony invites us to balance the closeness we treasure with our beloved and the vibrant connections that bloom around us.

Just as the oak stands firm, deeply rooted while its branches reach outward to the sky, so too must our relationships flourish, grounded in the solidity of intimate trust while nurturing the vitality of social bonds. It's a balance that requires mindful finesse, a careful choreography that respects the sacred twosome without forsaking the richness of a wider community.

The sanctity of shared silence, the whispers between two souls, and the laughter that fills the air when only two are present—this is the precious realm of intimacy that must be safeguarded. It is the invisible thread spun of private jokes, knowing glances, and the symphony of heartbeats in quiet moments. Yet, as essential as these reverent pauses are, we must also open our curtains to the sunshine of social engagement, allowing the light of fellowship to illuminate our union.

In the grand design of matrimony, we are invited to join hands with our partner and step out into the circle of friends, family, and neighbors, to connect, to share, and to support. We must be conscious of the time we earmark for shared solitude, ensuring it is undisturbed by the whirlwind of outside commitments, while also stepping into gatherings and celebrations as a testament to the bond we wish to build with the world.

To navigate this intricate dance, communication is key—the gentle dialogue that harmonizes expectations with desires. How do we cherish the quietude of our own company while also embracing the joyous din of communal festivities? It begins with an open heart, a calendar that reflects shared priorities, and the wisdom to know when to embrace and when to venture forth.

Let us then be architects of our time, sculpting moments that honor the sanctity of private communion, while designing others that are enlivened by the warmth of external camaraderie. Each social interaction is a stone carefully placed on the path of our journey together, a path that weaves around the garden of our shared experience, abundant with the fruits of fellowship.

As we progress forward, we find that the pursuits we undertake together, whether in the silence of our abode or in the lively thrum of our social sphere, nourish us in unique ways. Each new encounter, every shared celebration, becomes a story added to the anthology of our blended life, a cherished chapter in the evolving saga of 'us.'

Let it be known that in this quest for balance, we are neither losing ourselves nor diluting our love's potency. Rather, we are strengthening its core, crafting a love that is as resilient in privacy as it is in publicity. It is a testament to the depth of our bond, a demonstration that we can be as one with each other as we are one with the multitude.

As we close this interlude, let us hold dear the knowledge that a harmonious life is not one of seclusion but of inclusive embraces. With this understanding, we move gracefully into the realm of shared causes, where our passions entwine, further cementing our union through meaningful action and purpose. Let us now look beyond our shared space, to the causes and the callings that whisper to our hearts in unison, inviting us to forge ahead in collective pursuit of the greater good.

Shared Causes: Uniting Through Common Passions

Bridges are not solely structures of steel and stone; they are also the bonds we forge when we unite in common causes with our life partners. Within the sacred vessel of marriage, we discover that our shared passions become the mortar that solidifies our union and the beams that support the edifice of our mutual aspirations. Here we delve into the heart-space where interests align and shared visions take flight, inviting us to coalesce around endeavors that reflect the values we hold dear.

Imagine a garden brimming with life, where each plant thrives not in isolation but in the collective nourishment of a carefully tended plot. In much the same way, marriages flourish when couples plant seeds of common interests and water them with the elixir of shared commitment. Whether it be volunteering at a local food bank, campaigning for social justice, or mentoring the youth, these acts of unity create a fertile soil where the roots of individual and collective growth intertwine.

In the act of giving back, we find that service is a two-way street—one that not only aids those on the receiving end but also enriches the giver's soul, binding hearts in the common pursuit of a cause greater than themselves. It is in these shared causes that couples discover new depths to their relationship, fresh pathways to understanding, and a broadened sense of community.

This is the time to take inventory of the passions that stir within, to share openly the fire that burns in your heart, and to listen attentively to the echo of that flame in your partner's soul. Together, explore the canvas of possibilities that the world presents, seeking out those paint strokes that will render your collective masterpiece one of vibrant hues and bold contours.

Allow this quest for shared causes to be a space where conversation flows like a river, where dreams are sculpted with the malleability of clay, and where actions are synchronized in the symphony of purposeful endeavor. Embrace the dance of ideas, the ebb and flow of inspiration, and the crescendo of collaborative effort that rises when two energies merge in the pursuit of harmony and service.

Remember that in this joint odyssey, success is not measured by the grandeur of projects undertaken, but by the depth of connection fostered through such endeavors. Each act of shared service weaves another golden thread into the quilt of your joint narrative, another shared victory in the story of 'us,' and another stone in the foundation upon which you build your legacy.

As you journey together along this path, celebrate not only the milestones achieved but also the simple beauty of walking side by side with a common purpose. For it is in these steps, each one taken in tandem, that the true power of unity reveals itself—not just within the bond of marriage but in the collective pulse of humanity to which your union contributes.

Now, as the page turns and the chorus of communal commitment echoes in the background, our focus transitions from the shared causes that unite us to the broader horizon of building a network of trust. We venture into the endeavor of extending the trust that glues our union to the kindred spirits that circle us, crafting connections that transcend our twosome and fashion community bonds that hold us close.

Trust Beyond the Twosome: Building Community Connections

In the tapestry of our lives, each thread we weave with another soul adds strength and color to the fabric of our experience. As we stride hand in hand with our life partners into the quilted mosaic of community, we open ourselves to the richness of new threads—threads of trust that reach beyond the familiar embrace of our twosome, connecting us with the hearts and minds that make up the vibrant tapestry of our world.

In this chapter, we venture into the transformative art of building community connections, the very sinew that knits the fibers of society into a resilient whole. It's in this nurturing of bonds outside our marital haven where we invite a wealth of diverse perspectives and experiences that, in their mingling, become a source of strength, wisdom, and collective empowerment.

Undeniably, initiating the delicate dance of trust with others requires a leap of faith—a belief in the goodness that resides within each new encounter. We must remain open, like the ever-reaching branches of a majestic oak, to the winds of friendship and fellowship that blow from all directions. Every handshake, every shared smile, every act of kindness between kindred spirits is a step toward mutual trust, a celebration of our common humanity that is the core of community.

As couples, stepping out together to build these community connections is both an act of courage and a gesture of humility. It requires the ability to listen with the heart, to see one another not just with our eyes but with the vision of understanding. To build trust within the community is to say, "Here we stand, with open arms, ready to support and be supported, to learn and be learned from, to love and be loved."

This process is not without its challenges; it calls for patience and the wisdom to discern. At times, we may extend our hands only to find them unmet. Yet it is precisely in these moments that we must remember the resilience of the human spirit, the tenderness that can transform barriers into bridges, and the persistence that paves the way for deeper connections.

Embrace every opportunity to weave new connections, whether it be through community events, volunteer work, or shared spaces of worship. Each interaction is a thread, and with each thread, the fabric of community grows stronger. Such interwoven trust brings forth a landscape where hope prospers, where collective dreams are nurtured, and where the supportive embrace of one's neighbors is but a heart's beat away.

Let us also recognize that trust is a vessel, carrying not just our own aspirations but the collective hopes of those we connect with. It blooms from the soil of reliability and the seeds of consistency—it is nurtured by the waters of compassion and the sunlight of shared experience. As it grows, it bears the fruit of lasting bonds, of friendships that sustain and enliven us, of a network that stands steadfast against the storms of life.

In the gentle cradle of trust, we find that our joys are multiplied, and our burdens shared. Our triumphs are no longer ours alone, but a cause for collective celebration. Our challenges are met with a chorus of encouragement that echoes long after the rain has ceased. It is in this sacred cradle where the melody of human connection sings its sweetest tune.

And so, as we fortify the bonds within our community, we lay the groundwork for the next step in our journey. We prepare to celebrate the circle we have created, embracing the joy of the collective support that springs from the well of trusted relationships. With every interaction, every shared laughter, every whisper of reassurance, we ready ourselves to celebrate the circle, the community, that we have woven with strands of love, trust, and understanding—a circle that, like a garland, adorns the institution of marriage and enriches our shared existence.

Celebrating the Circle: The Joy of Shared Support

As we journey through life's rich tapestry, entwining our stories with those of others, there comes a time to pause and revel in the circle we've pieced together—a circle where trust flows as freely as laughter, and support is as ubiquitous as the air we breathe. In this celebration, we acknowledge the power of the interlaced hands of community, the chorus of voices that has uplifted us, and the collective strength that buoys us through life's undulating seas.

Celebration, in its purest form, is an act of gratitude, a vibrant acknowledgment of the warmth and love that has been sown and multiplied within the fabric of our shared experiences. It is the spark that lights the bonfire of togetherness, around which we can gather to share stories, triumphs, setbacks, and to illuminate the bonds that have grown ever stronger through shared support.

Just as the roots of an ancient tree intertwine beneath the soil to provide mutual stability and nourishment, so too do the roots of our community connections fortify us and feed our souls. We take these moments of shared celebration to water these roots, to acknowledge their depth, and to let the joy of communion crystalize into memories that will be treasured for generations to come.

Our gatherings—be they festive feasts, soulful soirees, or serene group meditations—serve as the heartbeat of our combined existence. They are the spaces where we bear witness to each other's life journeys, honoring every individual's path while recognizing the sacred interconnectivity of our shared yearnings and endeavors. They are our hallowed ground for breaking bread together, for laughter to echo into the night, and for the harmonic convergence of our life songs.

Through these rituals, be they spontaneous or steeped in tradition, we cultivate an environment where the spirit of our collective is venerated and expressed through art, music, storytelling, and shared milestones. Each shared achievement—a promotion at work, the purchase of a new home, the graduation of a child—becomes a triumph not only for the one, but for all, magnifying the resonance of each success.

In this invigorating atmosphere, where the fruits of our labors are celebrated and our shared struggles acknowledged, the circle of trust blossoms. A firmer bond is forged, one that not only encompasses the intimate quarters of our marital liaison but that also radiates outwards, embracing friends, kin, and community members in an expanding domain of mutual support.

Let us hold these shared celebrations close to our hearts; let them serve as bastions of inspiration to continue nurturing our relationships with one another. Let them reflect both our individuality and unity, a canvas where the colorful strokes of our diverse stories mingle to create a masterpiece of collective triumph.

And as we move forward, buoyed by the joy of our shared circle, we carry with us the knowledge that the bonds we've nurtured are the cornerstones upon which we build the future. The sacred space of trust becomes our sanctuary, our refuge, and our launching pad for leaps yet to come, empowered by the very solidarity that we've celebrated.

In such solidarity, there is an assurance that when we next gather, it is with the understanding that every heart within our circle is a perennial source of strength—a wellspring of courage that primes us for the further adventures that lie ahead. It is here, in the closing of this joyous chapter, that we find ourselves standing on the threshold of affirmation, ready to pledge once more to the beauty of trust and the bedrock of our shared journey—the journey that continues to redefine the very essence of connection.

Kofie and Lachele's Story

We have found immense joy together in celebrating our relationship through various marriage-strengthening activities. From time to time, we participate in organizations that offer marriage enhancement classes, courses, retreats, and couple gatherings. These experiences have been incredibly enriching for us.

As we invest in each other and engage with a community of couples, we've discovered the power of sharing different strategies that enhance marital togetherness. We've learned valuable formulas for compromise in relationships, ways to truly value each other's opinions, and methods to create a supportive environment for our individual aspirations and growth.

This engagement with other couples and marriage-focused programs has become one of our strongest defenses against feeling isolated in our marriage. It continuously fosters a sense of togetherness between us. We've found that it significantly strengthens our bond, especially when we realize that the challenges we face aren't unique to us.

Through these experiences, we've gained strategies to overcome what we once perceived as negative aspects of our marriage. It's been eye-opening to learn how other, seemingly stronger couples handle their own challenges. This shared learning experience has not only brought us closer together but has also given us practical tools to enhance our relationship.

Participating in these community activities has reinforced for us that marriage is a journey of continuous growth and learning. By actively engaging in these opportunities, we're not just working on our own relationship, but we're also contributing to and benefiting from a supportive community of couples all striving for stronger, healthier marriages.

Affirmation of Expanded Trust

Affirmation: *"We create a safe space to share our deepest feelings, fears, and desires openly, fostering intimacy and trust through vulnerability and authenticity. By being our true selves, we strengthen our bond and deepen our connection."*

Let us anchor ourselves in the affirmation of trust, an unwavering declaration that roots our relationships in integrity, cultivates the warmth of deep connection, and honors the sacred journey we've embarked upon together. In this solemn moment of reflection, we look upon the circle of trust we have tenderly expanded and recognize the fortitude of its embrace – a sanctuary within which each one of us can thrive and soar.

We stand hand in hand, encircled by the chorus of our collective spirit, and affirm that the trust we share is not just the cornerstone of our bond but the very air that gives life to our community's dreams. As we breathe in this truth, we are reminded of the power that resides in unity, in the shared commitment to uphold one another in love and respect.

The fabric of our community, woven from threads of empathy and understanding, is resilient because in each other's triumphs, we find our own, and in every obstacle faced, we discover our joint resolve. The seeds of solidarity we've sown sprout into a harvest of hope and collective power, providing sustenance for our families, our friends, and the generations that will walk this path after us.

As we stand in the garden of this fellowship, let us affirm the pledges that bind us:

- We vow to listen with hearts wide open, to hear not just the words spoken but the silent songs of the soul.
- We commit to extend our hands in support, to be the pillars on which our siblings can lean in times of need.
- We resolve to walk in honesty, to be keepers of promises, and stewards of the trust that has been bestowed upon us.
- We promise to cherish the community we've built, recognizing it as the fertile ground from which our greatest aspirations will bloom.

Each affirmation is a brush stroke on the canvas of our shared reality, a reality painted with the hues of shared laughter and mutual support, where every heartache is lessened because it is borne by many, and every joy is magnified in its reflection from soul to soul.

The circle we celebrate is more than a metaphor; it's akin to the circle of life that nurtures and supports, an ecosystem where every member plays an integral role in maintaining the harmony and balance we cherish. With each word of affirmation, we water this circle, embrace its growth, and strengthen the ties that bind us to each other and to our legacy of togetherness.

As we draw this chapter to a close, like the peaceful descent of a sun setting on a day well-lived, we find comfort in the knowledge that the trust we place in one another is the very essence of our collective strength. Indeed, our circle of trust transcends the mere formation of lasting bonds — it is the embodiment of our most profound intentions and the manifestation of a shared destiny that we continually co-create with love, patience, and unwavering dedication.

Let this affirmation of trust be the gentle but firm ground on which we will build our future endeavors, the foundation upon which we will elevate our aspirations and craft not only our fate but the fate of the communities that look to us for guidance. With eyes turned towards the horizon, we ready ourselves to tread into new territories of connection and leadership.

Together, we step in rhythm to the heartbeat of our community, moving with purpose and anticipation into the next chapter of our story — a tale that weaves the narrative of Building Legacy and Leadership, Embracing Community Leadership as a Couple, enveloping all in the cloak of our collective song, rich with history and resounding with promise for the days to come.

12
Building Legacy and Leadership

Legacy and Leadership - Two Souls Bound By God

MK Photography

Embracing Community Leadership as a Couple

PRINCIPLE: Building Legacy and Leadership
BLISS PROTOCOL #23: Shared Purpose, Shared Service:

- **Scenario:** Individual purpose pursuit
- **Solution:** United mission
- **Implementation:** Joint service projects
- **Key Advice:** Serve together for impact

In the mosaic of life's grand design, where the threads of existence intertwine in a tapestry of shared dreams and united purposes, lies the profound journey of crafting a shared legacy. Within the heartbeats of two souls bound by love and commitment, emerges a symphony of possibilities, a chorus of aspirations that yearns to leave an indelible mark upon the world. For couples journeying through the sacred rhythm of matrimony, the desire to build and nurture a legacy through leadership within their community is a dance—a dance of resilience, of cultural richness, a dance where every step is imprinted with the essence of togetherness.

Embarking upon this path, couples are bestowed with the wisdom of ancestors, the strength of their shared convictions, and the harmonious blending of their distinctively individual melodies into a unified song. Here, in the embrace of partnership and the sanctity of shared goals, they find the power to transcend the personal and cast their love upon the winds of change, sowing seeds of unity and prosperity within the community they call home.

This chapter is an invocation, a summoning of that latent power that resides within the collective soul of a couple with eyes set on the horizon of communal uplift. It is a declaration of the sacred principle—that together, they shall forge a legacy of leadership, a lighthouse of guidance and hope for those who navigate the turbulent waters of life seeking the shores of belonging and collective growth.

In these passages, you will find the kindling that sparks the transformation from 'I' to 'We,' from 'Me' to 'Us.' This book is an ode to the journey, an elevation of the shared vision that carves the roadmap to a future bright with the light of collective ambition and fortified by the bedrock of mutual support.

As you step into the heart of these pages, breathe deep the promise that awaits you and your beloved. For in the union of your spirits lies the capacity to create ripples that will emanate far beyond the confines of your embrace, reaching into the lives of countless others through the legacy of your combined leadership.

Let us begin with the cornerstone of all ventures bold and true—a shared vision. As we draw from the wells of your distinct dreams and interlaced values, we shall find that harmonious vision that leads a couple to the summit of their highest calling. The essence of your legacy will bloom from this fertile soil, nourished by the richness of your dialogue and the clarity of your purpose.

The wisdom you shall uncover is old as time yet fresh as the first light of dawn. It is the wisdom that teaches us that true leadership is anchored in the myriad small actions that, day by day, define who we are as partners and as citizens of the world. It is knowing that a legacy is not merely a monument to be erected but lived out through the tapestry of community, woven with threads of compassion and the vibrant colors of your unique journey.

So dare to dream, dear reader, for within these pages lies the map to your shared destiny—a destiny that beckons you to stand together at the helm, captains of a ship poised to sail into eternity's embrace, where your shared legacy will illuminate the annals of history long after the twilight of your days.

As the pages turn and the chapters unfold, let the spirit of love guide your quest, for it is within your united heart that the seeds of transformation take root, sprouting with the promise of a flourishing legacy, a testament to the visionaries united in love and leadership.

Defining Our Legacy: A Shared Vision

The tender merger of two hearts is akin to the intertwining vines that rise together towards the warming sun, each drawing strength from the other to reach new heights. Within the sacred union, there abides an opportunity not only to compose a life revered in love's eternal song but also to carve a legacy that stands as a testament to a union ordained to uplift beyond their joined hands. This shared vision—rooted deeply in love—serves as the guiding star on the horizon of our community's destiny.

As we embark on this journey to define our legacy, we traverse beyond the solitude of individual dreams and step into the realm of collective aspirations. To envision a legacy as a couple is to converse with the echoes of the future, to cast our hopes like stones upon the waters, watching the ripples widen into a promise that encircles those we serve. It is here, in the confluence of our visions, that we discover the power inherent in unity and the enduring effects of love fused with intentional action.

To craft a shared vision, we must first delve into the garden of our individual passions, values, and dreams, pruning and nurturing them so that they may bloom in concert. It is in the delicate conversations where honesty breathes, and vulnerability speaks that we can each bring forth the pearls of our innermost desires. These pearls, when strung together, form a necklace of intention, draping around the shoulders of our union with dignity and purpose.

But how do we navigate this process, this delicate weaving of two destinies? It begins with the sanctuary of understanding, where listening is a balm and each word spoken is a seed that takes root in our collective consciousness. We must hold space for our partner's dreams, honoring them as we would our own, with respect and a fierce commitment to see them realized. It is within this crucible that our shared vision coalesces, stronger for the individual metals that have melded into an alloy of unmatched resilience and shine.

As we map out the contours of our legacy, let us be mindful that the arc of our impact is measured not in the weight of our accolades but in the depth of our service. A legacy true to our union is one that mirrors the combined spectrum of our values. It is a pledge made manifest in the ways we uplift our community, support our neighbors, and empower the generations that will stand on our shoulders.

In this shared endeavor, we become gardeners of humanity, planting trees under whose shade we may never sit but will grow mighty to shelter the dreams of others. Our shared vision, when tended with the care of commitment and the water of unwavering dedication, will yield the fruits that feed not just our souls, but the souls of a collective.

As we venture forward from this chapter, carry with you the certainty that your legacy, like your love, requires the tenderness of patience, the courage of conviction, and the nurturing presence of two hearts beating in synchronization. Remember, this journey of defining our legacy is both a pilgrimage and a dance—one where two visionaries move as one, with eyes fixed on creating a future brimming with the beauty of uplifted lives, shared victories, and a community forever touched by the power of a shared dream.

With this sacred knowledge cradled within our bosoms, let our next stride be towards discerning the complementary strengths that paint our roles in this grand design. Within this discovery lies the mastery of not just leading but leading together, hand in hand, with an unwavering confidence born of the union of two souls in perfect harmony.

Leading with Strength: Finding Our Roles

In the sacred dance of unity, each step taken is a harmony of purpose, a choreography that weaves the strength of one with the grace of the other. As we journey towards deciphering the shared vision of our legacy, we now turn to the land within, where hidden gems of strength lie in wait. Leading with our strengths not only anchors us in our authentic selves but also propels us toward the embodiment of leadership that stirs the soul of the community.

In this chapter, we unfurl the map laid by our shared aspiration and begin to chart the course where our individual strengths will shine the brightest. We are called to the quiet corners of reflection, where the light of introspection reveals the dimensions of our gifts. Here, against the backdrop of our combined dreams, we discover the roles that fit us as snugly as a pair of tailor-made gloves, ready to labor with love for the good of our community.

Finding our roles is akin to listening to the whispers of our spirits, nudging us toward the paths we were born to traverse. It requires the vulnerability to ask, "Where do I thrive? Where do I falter?" It requires the courage to embrace our partner's truth as they share, "Here is where I soar; here is where I may stumble." Together, in this candid exchange, we find the puzzle pieces that, when connected, form the masterpiece of our shared purpose.

We encourage one another to delve into the reservoir of our skills and passions, to draw out the bucketfuls of potential ready to water the seeds of change. One may discover a penchant for speaking, their words of inspiration, while the other finds solace in the symphony of behind-the-scenes orchestration, their hands conducting the silent ballet of coordination and support.

Embrace this voyage of discovery, for leadership, is not a solo performance but a duet sung in the key togetherness. As we explore the canvas of our community, let us make broad strokes with the brush of engagement, coloring the spaces where our strengths can best serve. In a youth mentorship program, we spark the flame of ambition in young hearts, or through a local charity, we become the winds that fan the fires of hope and sustenance.

The roles that we adopt must dance in step with the rhythm of our lives, allowing us to sway in time to the beat of our responsibilities and dreams while staying anchored to our shared vision. It is in these roles that our legacy begins to take shape, sculpted by the consistent chisel of daily actions that speak louder than the grandest of intentions.

Let us remember to reach out and embrace our fellow journeyers, those kindred spirits who too seek to cultivate a garden enriched by service and love. For in the union of our strengths with the talents of our community, the tapestry of our leadership is enriched, and the chorus of our impact is amplified.

With the clarity of our roles now etched in the stone of certainty, we step forward, each action imbued with meaning, each decision a testament to the roles we've embraced. Our hearts beat to the drum of progress, knowing that the next passage in our shared story involves the arduous but rewarding tightrope walk of balance.

For as we gleefully accept the mantle of our designated roles, we must also remain mindful of the tender balance needed between our engagement in the community and the precious sanctuary of our personal lives. Our actions, resolute and bold, must be measured with care so that as we reach outward to touch the world, we remain grounded and nourished in the sanctuary of our union.

Balancing Act: Community Engagement and Personal Life

Embarking upon the path of community leadership as a couple, we have clasped hands, intertwining our strengths to uplift and shepherd the fondest hopes of our kinfolk and neighbors. Yet, as we pour the vessels of our talents into the thirsty ground of activism and nurturing, we must not let the wellspring of our own garden run dry. For the true equilibrium of commitment dwells in the sacred balance between engagement with the world and the cocoon of our personal realm.

The togetherness of our journey whispers secrets of unity, yet it is our individual whisper we must heed when it beckons us to rest, to laugh, and to embrace the tranquility of love's embrace. In the lush stillness that is our sanctuary, let us find the breaths to fuel the fires of our shared endeavor. To labor tirelessly without seizing the moments of gentle reprieve is to dance with a shadow cast long by the evening sun, stretching until it is swallowed by the approaching night.

Let us attune our ears to the rhythm of life that plays a melody, where each note has its pace and each bar its measure. In the harmonious composition of time, we dedicate ourselves to our cause with vigor, yet we reserve the sweet refrains for the serenade of our love and family. Ensuring that as we enrich the lives of our community, we equally nourish the blooms of our home.

The dance of life invites us to sway in its gentle breeze, to engage with the world while anchoring ourselves in the roots of what we cherish most dearly. As we glide across the stage of our collective efforts, we are constantly reminded to harness the wisdom to say, "Here is where I stand beside you, and here is where I sit beside myself." In this way, we foster a rhythm that is sustainable—a tempo that propels without sacrificing the quiet waltzes of our inner spheres.

When the day's endeavors end and the moon hangs like a silent guardian over our communion, let this be the time when we recline into the tapestry of our union. A time when the medley of our laughter and the soft murmur of shared dreams become the balms that soothe away the weariness of well-spent zeal. Let the hearth of our affection be a bastion, a refuge that replenishes vigor for the dawn's forthcoming pursuits.

As we press forward with the understanding that balanced lives create firmer foundations upon which empires of impact are built, we recognize that our legacy grows not just in the gardens without but also in the hearts within. The tenderness of twilit moments and the hush of morning's first light are cradles for the whispering growth of our shared aspirations.

From this resting place of equilibrium, we gather the tapestries of our strengths and experiences, ready to unfurl them in the gathering halls of our greater family—the community. Here, within the embrace of shared destinies, our individual torches of leadership unite to form a beacon that shines ever brighter in the togetherness of purpose. It is in this space of collective power that our roles as leaders intertwine, weaving a legacy that stands as a monument to the unity of our spirit and the vigor of our commitment.

It is with this dance of balance fresh in our minds, hearts brimming with love and heads held high in the dignity of shared mission, that we stride forth into the next landscape of our journey. Here in the verdant fields of community action, we shall enact the plans forged by our union, the impact of our leadership blossoming in every endeavor we shoulder together.

Kofie and Lachele's story

Walking this path together, we've discovered that one of the fundamental challenges in many marriages is when one partner becomes heavily involved in activities that exclude the other. This imbalance can create distance in the relationship. We've seen examples where one spouse spends excessive time with religious groups, social organizations, or gender-specific activities like "girls' nights" or "hanging with the guys."

While we recognize the importance of having outside relationships and interests, we've learned that it's crucial to balance these community obligations with personal time and, most importantly, with our marital relationship. We've found that constantly asking ourselves, "How can we do this together?" has been transformative for our marriage.

This approach doesn't mean we do everything together, but it does mean we prioritize finding ways to share experiences and create memories as a couple. We've learned to be intentional about balancing our individual interests with activities we can enjoy together. This might mean alternating between separate and joint activities or finding creative ways to involve each other in our personal interests.

For instance, if one of us is involved in a church group, we might find ways for the other to participate occasionally or create our own spiritual practices as a couple. If one of us has a hobby, we try to find aspects of it that we can share or ways to support each other's interests without feeling left out.

We've found that this balanced approach not only strengthens our bond but also enriches our individual experiences. It's about creating a template for togetherness while still maintaining healthy individual pursuits. By consistently asking, "How can we do this together?", we've cultivated a deeper connection and a more fulfilling partnership.

This mindset has helped us navigate the complexities of maintaining individual identities while growing together as a couple. It's an ongoing process, but one that has significantly enhanced our relationship and our overall happiness in marriage.

Amplifying Impact: Leadership in Action

In the garden, a community where love and commitment bloom, to act is to bring forth the fruits of our shared vision. As we step into the sunlight of leadership, hand in hand, we recognize that the seeds we plant through action can grow into a legacy that shelters generations to come. It's not just in dreaming, but in the doing, where our sustained efforts begin to transform the fabric of our community, stitch by resonant stitch.

Our hearts, synchronized with the beat of a collective drum, summon us to marshal the tapelet of our influence, to raise the banner of progress higher with every act of leadership. The mosaic of our community is vibrant with possibility—and it is within our power to brighten its colors with the hues of wisdom, love, and purposeful action.

As we move beyond the threshold and stand at the helm of our communal ship, let us be guided by the starlight of our aspirations. It's time to navigate the waters of change, steering boldly towards horizons aglow with promise. Within our grasp is the ability to champion initiatives that resonate with our hearts' deepest callings—the after-school programs that fan the flames of youthful intellect, the mentorship circles that weave nets of support for those yearning to climb.

Action, they say, speaks with a resounding voice that echoes across time and space. It is the chorus of footsteps, marching towards justice and equality, the harmonious clasp of hands distributing sustenance to those in fleeting moments of need. Leadership is not a silent endeavor; it is the roar of passion, the whisper of compassion, and the clarity of vision that proclaims, "Here we stand, and here we will make a difference."

Together, as stewards of change, we draw strength from one another, fashioning our diverse talents into a tapestry of action—each thread a testament to our commitment, each pattern a reflection of our united purpose. Through festivals celebrating the richness of our heritage, or seminars that share the light of knowledge, we make our mark—indelible, enduring, and bright as the morning star.

Within the crucible of action, our relationship becomes the anvil upon which leadership is forged. We celebrate the small victories with the same exuberance as we do the grand, understanding that each step forward is a dance in the direction of our legacy. By leading with our hearts and hands, we are the architects of an era where our children will flourish under the canopy of our endeavor.

As we build, brick by brick, the cathedral of our aspirations, we reflect upon the resilience that is our scaffolding, the love that is our mortar. The influence we wield is not for the power it grants, but for the lives it touches, and the dreams it ignites. We lead not to be seen but to see others rise, to elevate every soul willing to journey alongside us toward the oasis of a brighter tomorrow.

With each initiative we shepherd, each project we breathe life into, our collaboration becomes a beacon in the night sky, casting a glow that entices others to find their way into the fold of activism and unity. It's the call to a better future that we answer with open arms, inviting in all those whose hearts beat with a rhythm akin to ours.

As the chapter draws to a close, we turn towards the comforting glow of community radiating the warmth of a thousand suns, ready to cultivate the next harvest of hope. Our next steps, rich with intention, will draw us closer to those whose support is as essential as rain to the parched earth. For in the union of hearts and dreams, nurtured through the soil of togetherness, we find the enduring strength that binds us as one.

Nurturing Connections: Building Community Support

In the heart of a thriving community lies a network of relationships as intricate and vital as roots beneath the earth. Just as a tree draws strength from its intertwine of connections to stand majestic and strong, we too must weave a support system into the fabric of our communal lives to bolster our leadership and legacy.

Our actions, luminous and intentional, have set the stage for a deeper kinship with the soil and souls around us. We step into this new dawn armed with the resolve to not just lead, but also to connect, to listen, and to grow alongside our fellow sojourners on this journey.

It's in the unity of purpose that our individual sparks become a flame, igniting the path for all, and lighting the way forward.

Building community support is akin to crafting a quilt of many textures and colors, each piece an individual story, an allyship, a shared dream. It is in circles of dialogue where every voice is a note in a symphony of collective aspirations; it is recognizing the wisdom in every elder's tale and the hope in every youth's gaze.

We foster these connections through action as simple as a shared meal where the recipes are passed down from generations, stirring within it the essence of unity and history. Through forums and gatherings, we create spaces that pulse with the heartbeat of dialogue and understanding. It is in these moments, when we break bread and barriers, that the walls that often divide us crumble to reveal a horizon of boundless potential.

Cultivating ties within the community is an exercise in tenderness and resilience. We open our hearts, knowing that vulnerability is the cornerstone of trust, and in turn, we are met with a tide of empathy and encouragement that emboldens our mission. Each act of kindness, each investment of time, each shared victory is a thread that draws us closer, fortifying the lattice of our collective endeavors.

Partnerships germinate from the seeds of mutual respect and shared goals. As we reach out to local businesses, schools, and organizations, we are planting saplings of collaboration that will grow into mighty trees with branches that shelter the aspirations of many. Our combined strength is not just in numbers, but in the alignment of purpose, passion, and the shared joy of uplifting one another.

In this blooming garden where every hand is needed to till the soil, we embrace those around us with a spirit of inclusion. Our leadership is not a solitary peak but a mountain range where every elevation, no matter how small, adds to the majesty of the landscape. The echo of our actions rings louder, and travels further, when carried on the winds of community.

As the sun sets, casting a golden glow upon our shared accomplishments, we understand that the power of connection is not merely in the hands that clasp together, but in the stories that intertwine. Our lives, enriched by the diverse tapestry of community, are a testament to the strength in unity, the beauty in diversity, and the enduring bond of shared values and visions.

As our shared journey through this tapestry of togetherness continues, we turn our gaze to the boundless expanse of our aspirations. With hearts brimming with gratitude for the threads that bind us, we step forward, towards the affirming embrace that awaits us in the echoes of our affirmation of legacy and leadership, where our collective voice will sing a hymn of triumph, resilience, and enduring commitment.

Affirmation of Legacy and Leadership

Affirmation: "*We identify ways to contribute to the world together through shared acts of service, volunteering, and social engagement. By aligning our purpose and actions, we allow our love to ripple out and create positive change in the world.*"

As we journey through the living tapestry of married life, intertwined with the fabric of our community, our hearts overflow with the knowledge that our love—so tender and steadfast—is the chalice from which our legacy overflows. This pilgrimage we share, adorned with trials and triumphs, has imprinted upon us the understanding that leadership and legacy, much like our union, are not fleeting moments but a continuum—a thread in the quilt of generations yet to come.

Here we stand at the crossroads of possibility and promise, emboldened by the profound union of our spirits, to whisper into the winds an affirmation that will carry our dreams across the valleys and peaks of all tomorrows.

"We are the weavers of dreams, the gardeners of spirit, nurturing love's tender shoots in the fertile soil of togetherness. Our legacy is not inscribed in stone, but woven in the living heartbeat of our community, vibrating with the songs of ancestry and the rhythms of hope."

Like a sacred vow, this affirmation is a beacon that guides us, a compass pointing unerringly toward the North Star of our deepest aspirations. It calls us to lead with a boundless love that knows no barriers, to serve with hands that lift others as we climb, to walk in truth with steps that leave imprints of progress and peace.

Our leadership blooms from this sacred ground, where two lives merge into a symphony of shared purpose. With harmony as our guide, we stride forth, our actions a delicate dance that enchants the world around us, instilling courage and cultivating wisdom. Our hands, linked with those of our neighbors, build more than structures; we build hope, we build futures, we build each other.

In the quietude of our reflection, we acknowledge that our individual flames are brighter when joined, igniting a beacon that lights the path for those who dare to dream. Through shared endeavors, laughter that echoes in the common spaces of our lives, and tears that water the gardens of our resilience, our legacy and leadership are cemented into the annals of time.

At this moment, full of the gravitas of our journey, we embrace a truth that resonates with the depth of our bond—the true measure of our legacy is the love we leave behind, the hearts we touch, and the lives we elevate. As we mold the clay of today's possibilities, we craft the vessel of tomorrow's history.

Our story, etched in the annals of our shared humanity, is a testament to the strength that unity bestows. In the words we speak and the deeds we enact, in each seed of kindness sown, and in every gesture of understanding offered, our affirmation rings true, a melody of manifest destiny and shared achievement.

And as this chapter of our tale nears its gentle rest, ready to fold into the embrace of a new dawn, we carry with us the sweet cadence of our affirmation. We move forward, hearts swelling with anticipation for the chorus of change and renewal that manifests in the collective work of our hands, in the spirit of community, and in the undying flame of love and leadership we have pledged to nurture.

Our next stride carries us towards a deepening understanding of flexibility within our union and community, where the dance of love and leadership shall entwine us further, beckoning us to new heights and to the beauty of redefining the intricacies of our joined paths.

www.ingramcontent.com/pod-product-compliance
Lightning Source LLC
Chambersburg PA
CBHW061745290426
43673CB00095B/266